The Cross and the Bomb

The Cross and the Bomb

*Christian Ethics and the
Nuclear Debate*

edited by
Francis Bridger

MOWBRAY
LONDON & OXFORD

Typeset by Fourjay Typesetters Ltd, Oxford
Printed in Great Britain by Redwood Burn Ltd. Trowbridge

Contents

CONTRIBUTORS

General Sir Hugh Beach is Warden of St George's House, Windsor Castle. During his military service he held a number of commissions and appointments in West Germany and at the Army Staff College, Camberley, and held the post of Master General of the Ordnance.

The Revd Dr Francis Bridger is lecturer in social theology and ethics at St John's College, Nottingham. He read history at Oxford and theology at Bristol, and has written a number of articles on theology and political issues. *The Cross and the Bomb* is his first book.

The Revd Richard Harries is Dean of King's College, London. He is the author of seven books, including *Should a Christian Support Guerillas?* (Lutterworth), and *The Authority of Divine Love* (Blackwell). He edited and contributed an essay on the morality of deterrence to *What Hope in an Armed World?* (Pickering and Inglis).

Fr Gerard Hughes, SJ is head of the philosophy department and lecturer in ethics at Heythrop College, London. He is the author of *Authority in Morals* (Sheed and Ward).

The Rt Revd and Rt Hon. Dr Graham Leonard is Bishop of London. For seven years until March 1983 he was Chairman of the General Synod Board for Social Responsibility. In that capacity, he introduced the debate on Nuclear Arms in the General Synod in February last. He is now Chairman of the General Synod Board of Education. His writings have largely been concerned with Pastoral Theology.

The Revd Prof. Ulrich Simon is Professor Emeritus of London University where he held a chair in Christian Literature and was Dean of King's College. Among his books, *Theology of Auschwitz* and *Sitting in Judgment* (SPCK) are relevant to *The Cross and the Bomb*.

The Revd Prof. Keith Ward is F.D. Maurice Professor of Moral and Social Theology, King's College, London, and a director of the Centre for Law, Medicine and Ethics. He has written numerous books on philosophy, theology and ethics, the most recent of which is *Rational Theology and the Creativity of God* (Basil Blackwell).

ACKNOWLEDGEMENTS

The editor wishes to thank Group Captain Leonard Cheshire VC for permission to quote from his lecture *The Error of Pacifism* in chapter 1, and Times Newspapers Limited for permission to use in chapter 3 an extract from Bernard Levin's interview with Alexander Solzhenitsyn published in the *Times* on 23 May 1983.

INTRODUCTION
Francis Bridger

This book originated as a response to the Anglican report *The Church and the Bomb*. Since its inception, however, it has grown from a particular reply to a particular report into a larger discussion of the moral case for multilateralism.

Three reasons make this significant. Firstly, since the NATO decision of 1979 to modernize nuclear systems in Europe, the renewed rise of unilateralism has contained a vocal Christian element which has presented its stance as the only legitimate one for Christians to follow. This has been reinforced by a flow of theological publications and public declarations by churches. The present authors seek to refute this claim by arguing a case which they believe to be no less moral, but which points in the direction of deterrence and multi lateralism.

Secondly, since the unilateralist argument is frequently presented as morally self-evident, it seemed important to subject such a claim to detailed scrutiny. The structure and content of this symposium are thus concerned primarily with moral theology, but not exclusively so. Insofar as moral theology is an empirical subject, as Gerry Hughes has argued in chapter two, it is important that any claim to ethical judgment on the nuclear issue be informed by factual information. In providing an explanation of the strategy of deterrence, General Sir Hugh Beach and Mr Michael Quinlan have contributed such information. Since many Christians and non-Christians alike misunderstand or ignore this aspect, these contributions are highly pertinent.

Over the months, however, the debate has thrown up some central theological and moral themes. These are taken up by the Bishop of London in his essay which sets the agenda for what follows: the morality of pacifism, the concept of submission as a Christian virtue, the relevance of just war theory, the significance of power, the problem of method in moral reasoning. All are elaborated and argued through at greater length in subsequent chapters.

Finally, what of the contributors? We come from a wide variety of backgrounds and vocations. Our essays are ecumenical in that uniting round a central theme they bring insights from traditions ranging from Evangelical Anglicanism through Catholic Anglicanism to Roman Catholicism. We do not agree at all points, but we are at one in the belief that the issue of nuclear arms is perhaps the most critical facing the present generation. We are also convinced that for the thoughtful Christian, unilateralism is not the only moral option, and that powerful arguments may be adduced to suggest the opposite.

St John's College, Nottingham   FRANCIS BRIDGER
June 1983

1
A FRAGILE PEACE
Graham Leonard

1. A fragile peace

It is commonly stated, particularly in discussions of the appalling prospect presented by the experience of nuclear weapons, that the most urgent problem facing mankind today is the preservation of peace. While no Christian would, I hope, deny the moral obligation which rests upon us to do all that we can to avoid conflict and to work for peace, to put all the emphasis on the absence of conflict, as if to assert that it is the chief end of man, is, I believe, quite inadequate and misleading. In the first place 'peace' can mean very different things to different people. Lenin, the real architect of modern Marxism, for example, said that 'as an ultimate objective, peace simply means communism would control'. More important, it fails to give proper regard to the nature of man and the purpose for which he is created.

The account in scripture of the saving acts of God in history, beginning with the call of Abraham and ending with the record of the Church proclaiming the Gospel in the power of Pentecost, is set within a Prologue provided by the first eleven chapters of Genesis and an Epilogue provided by the book of Revelation. The former sets the context in which the saving acts take place. The latter presents the end point for which creation exists.

In the Prologue in Genesis, certain basic characteristics of man are established. He is given the power of choice whether to obey God or not. That choice involves the recognition of the difference between good and evil. The exercise of that choice in a way which does not accord with the will of God has the gravest consequences. Man is isolated from God and from his fellow men. Conflict arises and man is pictured as trying to build for himself a civilization which would justify itself apart from God and the result of which is chaos and confusion. Man who as vicegerent of creation is called upon to express the praises of creation to its Creator finds himself in a world which was 'corrupt before God' and 'filled with violence'. It is in that context that man is still called upon to exercise his power of choice, discerning what is good and what is evil and cleaving to the good.

The Prologue also speaks of God, who in spite of man's misuse of the freedom with which he was created, seeks to restore man to fellowship with himself. He does so in a way which respects man's freedom and does not therefore deliver man from the natural consequences of his decisions. It is significant that the delivery of Noah and his family from the flood is not achieved by a miraculous change in the natural destructive power of water but by an invitation to make provision for salvation in a way which reflects other properties of water, that is by the making of the ark. In other words, the natural order of creation is given as a framework in which man is free to exercise his freedom and he cannot expect creation to be modified to relieve him of the consequences of the exercise of his power of choice.

In the Epilogue of Revelation we are given a vision of the ultimate purpose for which creation exists. It is the gathering together of all things in one in Christ. The whole of creation, freed from the bondage of corruption, perfectly fulfils itself and does so to the glory of God. Man takes his place in expressing the praise of creation as it reflects back to God his holiness. But it also makes clear in the most dramatic way that this can only be achieved by the defeat of evil, with which there can be no compromise. The victory of Christ, the Lamb that was slain, has to be implemented to the full before the End of the Ages when the nations will dwell in peace in the City of God. Scripture gives us every ground for hope in Christ and in his death and resurrection, but it gives no warrant for supposing that in the last resort all will be done in a way which confuses good with evil and blurs the difference. Between the Prologue and the Epilogue, man exists in a fallen world: in Old Testament times with the promise of salvation and since Pentecost with salvation achieved but still to be implemented. In both ages he exists in a world which, being disordered, needs an authority to restrain, an authority which must ultimately be backed by power to secure justice and freedom. Neither in the Old nor New Testaments is such authority condemned in itself. On the contrary in the Old Testament the authority and power of Cyrus, King of Persia, was, for example, used by God in the preparation of the people of Israel for the coming of Christ; in the New Testament the authority of Caesar is recognized both by Our Lord and in the Epistles. St Paul makes it clear in Romans 13 that one of its functions is to witness to the distinction between good and evil and to help man to be true to his moral nature. The readers of 1 Peter are told to use the freedom which government provides as bondservants of God and not for a cloak of wickedness. The recognition and acceptance of authority carries with it recognition and acceptance of the power which is its ultimate sanction.

What does this say to us who have to live in a world which is still corrupt and full of violence, and in which by his ingenuity man has made the ultimate sanctions of power and human authority of such horrifying nature and with such appalling consequences, that he cannot bear to contemplate their use?

TWO ALTERNATIVES

Given that situation, there are, I believe, two alternatives. The first is to say that nuclear weapons as devised by man are of such evil nature in themselves that their possession and use can never be justified whatever the circumstance. If we adopt that line then we must be very clear as to its implications for they are very far reaching indeed. As the report, *The Church and the Bomb*[1] recognizes, 'nuclear weapons can never be disinvented. Their possibility is with us forever'. It would mean, therefore, that for all time, the power to exercise authority would in the last resort, be with those who had no inhibitions about its use. Is this position which is essentially that of the pacifist morally defensible?

The alternative course is to accept that in a fallen world there must be authority which is backed by the ultimate sanction of force if nations and people are to be dissuaded or prevented from acting in ways which are both morally wrong and injurious to their fellow human beings, and if individuals are to be free to act in accordance with their consciences. This is essentially the way of deterrence.

Before examining each of these positions in detail it must be pointed out that in practice, neither of these two positions has been followed with complete logic. The pacifist does not reject all authority which, since it must in the last resort have the sanction of force, would be the logical results of his beliefs. I have not, for example, met a pacifist who declines to take advantage of the police force, who is not content to benefit from the conditions provided by his local authority, or who objects to calling upon the courts in any matter. Yet both rely in the last resort upon the use of force to implement their actions. Likewise the advocate of deterrence has never maintained that in all circumstances where an evil is threatened or precipitated, force must be used to assert the moral law, allay the threat or remedy the injustice. The use of force has always been subject to certain checks and safeguards and, in certain circumstances, the possible results of using force would be likely to be such as to outweigh the moral benefit. The concept of the just war is an example of how mankind has sought to define these circumstances.

The reason for this is not simply lack of determination or moral courage. I believe that it springs from the fact that we live in a world in which human beings are free to choose between good or evil and do not always choose the good. In seeking to act in accordance with our moral nature, we cannot behave as if everyone chose the good or as if everyone chose the evil. Our decisions have always to take account of the fact that all human beings, including Christians, are moved by conflicting motives: by love, loyalty, and compassion on the one hand, for example, and by envy, bitterness, and greed on the other. As a result, any attempt to live by the former has to recognize the demands put by the latter. To take the example of the command to love our neighbour, perfect love is the offering and receiving of unblemished goodwill. My lack of holiness and the evil within me means that my goodwill to the person I love is marred by selfishness, pride, and so on. This also means that if the person whom I love is to return to me what is best for me, it must contain within it an element of judgement, offered, one hopes, in goodwill. For if the person whom I love condones what is wrong in me, he gives me something other than goodwill. There must be an element of 'law' as well as 'gospel' in our relationship. So if I have betrayed my friend, his love for me must confront me with my betrayal, as a means of our true reconciliation. For him simply to accept it within himself as if I had never betrayed him would be false to us both. What matters, of course, is that in confronting me he is moved by goodwill not by self-righteousness, reproachfulness or bitterness. So if a mother discovers her child stealing, her true love must include reproof based on recognition of the nature and consequences of the act. So also in the case of feeding the hungry, the moral demand to provide for their need must take account of the moral demand to encourage human responsibility. This requires action in respect of those who determine the use of resources and the provision of work and the encouragement of those in need to respond to such remedies as are made available. Merely to feed the hungry without taking account of these factors serves to perpetuate the distinction between 'haves' and 'have nots' and undermines human freedom and responsibility. As Richard Harries, Dean of King's College, London, says, 'Part of the way we show our love for our enemy is by not letting injustice succeed'.[2] But just as the goodwill must contain the element of judgement, so the element of judgement must be tempered by goodwill. It must have as its purpose the evoking and growth of moral goodness. Condemnation of evil itself with no active course for reformation, the restoration of relationship or the encouragement of the good, is purely sterile and in fact only feeds self-righteousness with its own destructive power.

From this it follows that in a fallen world, with the confusion of good and evil, no one moral imperative can be applied without considering it in relation to others. It may be argued in response that the command to love includes and provides for all other moral imperatives. This may be so if the command to love is understood in its strict and not a popular and sentimental sense. But it does not invalidate the argument that love so defined involves the fulfilment of the demand to recognize and encourage and respond to what is good, and the demand to judge and take account of what is evil.

GOVERNMENT AND POWER

What I have said about the situation at the personal level applies even more and in a somewhat different way at the corporate level. Because of the fallen nature of man, government with the power to enforce its demands, is necessary and inevitable. 'It is the result of and a remedy for our limited capacity to take other people into account'.[3] The moral demands laid upon a corporate body with responsibility for a group are twofold. In the first place it has responsibility for the continued existence of the group. This means that it is not free to sacrifice its own

9

interests in the way that is possible for an individual. The difference between the way in which groups relate to each other as compared with individuals has again been put very clearly by the Dean of King's College, London:

'Groups do not relate to one another in the same way as individuals do. The main difference lies in the fact that when relating to another individual I am dealing with someone who can, if he wishes, forego his own interests in favour of mine. Someone walking down a towpath and seeing me drowning can decide to dive in to rescue me even at considerable risk to himself. But when two groups relate to one another neither is in a position to sacrifice its essential interests. Furthermore, those who are elected to office in each group will be elected because it is widely judged that they are the persons who will pursue the interests of the group most effectively. There is nothing reprehensible in itself about this. It operates at every level of society and is quite natural. A school, for example, will want to employ the best teachers, build the finest facilities and produce students who have begun to develop their potential. A headmaster is appointed because the governing body believes he will be the person best able to develop the life of the school along these lines. It would be inappropriate for a headmaster to give away his laboratories and allow others to hire his best teachers out of a sense of altruism. But what happens whenever human beings organize themselves into groups, takes on a tragic dimension when those groups are nations. Conflicts over territory, national prestige, political ideology and vital raw materials occur against the background of mutual power to devastate. Yet the same principles apply as in any organized group life. People elect the government they think will best safeguard and strengthen the interests of the nation. They would regard it as highly inappropriate if a Prime Minister started to give away oil fields or disband the army when faced with bellicose statements by a potential aggressor. The tragic element in this is most starkly obvious in the quality of patriotism. Patriotism has called out some of the highest qualities known to man; but those same qualities have made it possible for nations to destroy each other in the most futile wars.'[4]

The first requirement laid upon a government is one which is accepted by any state. It is clearly accepted by the USSR but the basis on which it is accepted is significantly different. In saying this I am not referring to the purpose for which the USSR accepts it. Some argue that fear and a concern for survival is the dominant motive of the Soviet government in seeking to maintain superior military power. Others argue that though this is undoubtedly a strong element in its attitude, the oft-repeated aim of Marxism-Leninism to achieve world communist domination must be taken at its face value and the maintenance of the Soviet Republic and its satellites would be seen as a necessary prerequisite. The difference to which I want to draw attention is that of the underlying basis on which the state is to be preserved. As Mr Harries makes clear in the last sentence of the passage which I have quoted, the moral ambiguity of man means that even in a democratic society, patriotism can become corrupted and be used to serve evil ends.

WESTERN VALUES

The Christian, and, I would suggest, anyone who believes in the traditional values of western civilization, must be concerned to ensure that such values are the basis on which the State exercises its responsibility to protect the interests of the nation. This is vital for both internal and external reasons. It is vital if within the nation liberty is to be preserved, the rights of minority respected, and conflicts of interest channelled so that these do not become violent. It is vital if in pursuing its national interest on the international scene, it is to base its actions on the same principles as apply within the state. The need for the establishment of some form of international code is urgent but it would be disastrous if it were established on the basis of a denial of those beliefs about the nature and destiny of man which are embodied both in natural law and in the Gospel. We must not shut our eyes to the fact that Communist control means the repudiation of natural as well as Christian morality. It means that the State, not God, who is Love, Holiness and Goodness, determines what is right and wrong. It means the suppression of those who dissent and psychiatric prison to correct their dissident opinions.

The late Archbishop T. D. Roberts SJ, who was an advocate of non-violent resistance, had no doubts about the difference in morality between Communist values and that which he described as 'values fundamentally Christian'. 'The conditioned communist has no problem here at all, whether to wipe out a hundred million people with H-bombs is no more of a *moral* problem than the liquidation of the millions in the Ukraine or in China. One question alone is relevant: "Will this help to establish world communism?" The west is by comparison weighed down with cumbersome armour. "Should we use this means to repel communism?" is open to a hundred different answers for a hundred free people because the western tradition suggests at least the possibility of a God to whom man is responsible and whose image is one who never stooped to the method of his enemies.' 'Yet,' he continues, 'we must resist evil,'[5] and writes of resistance by non-violent means.

I suggest that in moving so quickly to the resisting of evil, he is leaving out a stage in the process which is essential both on principle and in practice. The second of the two moral demands laid upon a state is to witness to and to preserve the values upon which the society it is committed to preserve exists. This is necessary for internal government which, again because of the nature of man, will have to involve some measures of compulsion and restraint. Not only must the intention of such measures be made clear. The evidence of publicly declared intentions, as for example, by a constitution, or by a framework in which the authority of a democratically elected assembly operates, provides a constant check against the erosion of liberty and the development of tyranny. In the external relations of the state to other countries, it means that the purpose of its national defence policy is seen to ensure not merely survival but the preservation of those values which are regarded as essential both for a healthy and morally good society at home and for an international order. It may well be argued that public declarations of foreign policy are received with a certain amount of cynicism and suspicion, and there is an element of truth in this. It is never easy to convince anyone simply by professing one's intentions that they are good and that one will act upon them whatever the circumstance. It is however, quite a different matter for a state to act in such a way as to imply that the moral basis of society is not a matter of principle, and to proclaim by these actions that it is content for the ultimate sanction in international relations to be in the hands of those who deny the claims of the moral law.

It is therefore necessary before considering ways in which evil can be resisted if it materializes in positively hostile form to consider first how a nation can and should make it clear that there are moral norms which it regards as non-negotiable. To fail to do so can have the effect of encouraging those who have no moral scruples and for whom moral considerations are irrelevant to pursue their aims, and thereby endanger not only peace in the limited sense of the absence of conflict but human freedom as well.

PACIFISM AND DETERRENCE

We must now return to the consideration of the two ways of pacifism and deterrence. I appreciate that pacifism is a term which covers a wide range of views: I use it in the strict sense to describe that view which denies the right ever to take up arms even if one's country or oneself is threatened with subjugation or extinction.

I fully accept that there are those who believe that they have a vocation to embrace this position and must in conscience do so. I respect them and I believe that they have a significant role to play in the world not unlike that played by monks or nuns in the Christian Church. By their vows of poverty, chastity and obedience they witness in their total dedication to the element of those qualities which should be found in the life of every Christian. Not every Christian, however, has the vocation to embrace them wholly in the way that a monk or nun is called to do. Indeed, not only would the life of human society become unworkable but after the passage of time the human race would cease to exist. So I see the true pacifist as called to remind us all of the way in which violence should be eschewed in every aspect of human life and witnesses to it by his or her way of life.

But I find great difficulty when pacifism is advocated as a policy which should be adopted by those who have the responsibility of government.

In the first place, if the weak and powerless are to be protected the exercise of power is essential, and the role of the pacifist must be limited to acting as a cleansing influence in the exercise of this power. It is very difficult to see how the moral obligation to work for justice and freedom for the oppressed could be fulfilled if pacifism were adopted as the basis of national or international policy.

Secondly, pacifism requires the willingness to suffer. In fact, it steals a march on power by allowing it to demonstrate the limited extent of what it can achieve. But in the process the pacifist must be prepared to suffer. He or she has every right to accept that for himself or herself and if conscience so directs it must be obeyed. But I do not believe that it is morally right because of that conviction to require suffering on the part of those who do not share it. To do so seems to me to be guilty of acquiescing in violence being done to others. For this reason I cannot accept that pacifism is the way of establishing peace and international security. The very word 'pacifist' seems in fact to be a misnomer. A more accurate term for the strict pacifist viewpoint would be 'non-resistance to evil by physical means', for pacifism does not bring peace either in the sense of absence of conflict or of harmony. What it offers is the prospect of being subjugated without resistance or possiblity of annihilation.

A further objection to pacifism as a policy is that it elevates the moral demand not to take up arms in such a way that other moral demands, such as those presented by justice or truth, have not merely to take second place but have no place at all. It would therefore, be a declaration by the West that rather than resist the attempted enforcement of say, the amoral and irreligious belief of the USSR, or Nazism, it would acquiesce in them as a move of secondary importance compared with the one need to avoid taking up arms.

In recent years a particular form of pacifism has emerged which can be described as nuclear pacifism, that is the view that while it is possible to acquiesce in the use of conventional weapons, horrific though they are, nuclear weapons are so evil and have such evil consequences that they must be abandoned at all costs.

This view shares all the difficulties presented by traditional pacifism for if any form of force is accepted, it is that which presents the ultimate sanction which really matters. Even if attempts were made to restrict war to the use of conventional weapons, nuclear weapons or their possibility would always remain and could be used for blackmail.

14

This view does however introduce another difficulty to which I have already referred briefly. It takes the line that whereas the kind of limitation and control envisaged in the Just War Doctrine may make the use of conventional weapons just tolerable, nuclear weapons are so evil that no such restriction or control could make them morally acceptable. Nuclear pacifism therefore is prepared to accept that the ultimate power in the world, which on its own definition is inherently evil, should be wholly in the control of those who have no scruples about the possession or use of such weapons. This I find an argument which is morally very questionable. The fact that something evil exists which amoral men are prepared to use does not release me from the obligation to try and control its use, and justify a refusal to have anything to do with it.

NON-VIOLENT RESISTANCE

Also in recent years, the view has been propounded that the way to deal with an aggressor would be to submit and accept occupation but to make the country ungovernable by a deliberate policy of non-cooperation and non-violent resistance. I can do no better than quote what Group Captain G. L. Cheshire, VC has said about this proposal:

'The proposal should not be lightly dismissed, for it is put forward by men of high intelligence and, for the most part, of deep religious conviction. Their motive derives from the argument that the world has been fighting for the last 7,000 years without solving its problems and that therefore an alternative solution should be sought. But when confronted with the hard facts of human and historical reality, it is almot impossible to see how any such policy could conceivably work.

Gandhi, to whom appeal is made, did undoubtedly achieve some success with these methods. But he himself stated, as have his followers very consistently ever since, that his success depended upon the fact that his adversary – Britain – lived by a set of moral values and "adhered to the rule of the game". With a Hitler it would be an entirely different matter. The proponents of the argument themselves claim that there would be needed forceful leadership, efficient co-ordination throughout the country and a very high sense of dedication. The potential Hitler however would have no scruples whatsoever in the methods he adopted and appropriate counter-measures would be well within his capacity. Leaders, key personnel, indeed anyone capable of causing him difficulty, would disappear during the night, never to be seen again. The victim State would be denied all means of communication and if food was short it would be the inhabitants, not the occupying force, who would be deprived first. Intimidation would be used against some, and enticement to collaborate against others, and history shows only too well how easily collaborators come forward. It is inconceivable that in the long term any form of organized resistance would be left still remaining, except perhaps against small groups, highly dedicated no doubt but with no power of morally influencing the occupying force. The only opposition that ever bothered Hitler was the Resistance whose principal weapons were sabotage and armed guerilla tactics.

There is one other point too. For the proposal to work, the majority of the nation would have to endorse it. The Government would then need to declare publicly that such was its policy and set about disbanding all the armed forces, unless it were hypocritical enough to maintain a military potential with no intention of ever using it. If this were once done, the door would be open to any aggressor, however small, who cared to take advantage of the situation. One would further have to ask, in view of our integration into the NATO alliance, what would be the repercussions on our Allies?

So in the contemporary scene I simply cannot see, either from the point of view of fundamental Christian principle or on practical grounds that the non-violent resistance plan of the pacifist is viable.'[6]

Pacifism is based on the forswearing of force. Deterrence in some form, which is the only alternative way of attempting to deal with human conflict, is based on the control of force by so directing its use that its worst effects are prevented. The system of law and order operating in civilized society is based on this principle and is a form of deterrence. Force with the authority of the state is used to prevent the exercise of force in ways which are harmful to society or to individuals. As well as restraining those who so act and dissuading them from doing so, it has two other functions. First, it makes evident that there is a moral basis to society, and secondly, it encourages the resolution of differences by dissuasion or regulation rather than by people taking the law into their own hands. Force is used under the control of the law which provides among other things that the sanctions permitted are proportionate to the offences which they are intended to prevent. If they are either too severe or too mild they will not have their intended effect and the law will fall into disrepute. What matters is that, in the last resort, the law is capable of being enforced. If it is not, uncontrolled force will take over and might rather than right will prevail as the basis of society.

GOOD VERSUS RIGHT?

I have spoken of the control of force by law. In that process, we come face to face with the fact that it is frequently necessary to perform acts which it would be difficult to describe as morally good but which in the particular circumstance are right and permissible. Thus it can be right and permissible for a police officer to shoot a person when seeking to enforce the law and in self-defence. The purpose of his action is not simply to defend himself. It is part of the process of demonstrating that the moral sanctions of society must be obeyed. His action cannot be described as morally good but it can, and I believe, must be defended as right and morally permissible. Such actions must themselves be constantly subjected to moral criteria, hence the strict controls in this country on the use of firearms by the police and the outcry when they appear to be disregarded. Likewise, the sanctions which society applies are, or should be, constantly reviewed on moral grounds. So it is that in this country the death penalty has been abolished.

The fact is that we do not live in an ideal world, in which the choices before us always present the possibility of actions which are morally good. Frequently we find ourselves in situations in which none of the options open to us are wholly good and all have elements in them which we deplore. Such situations arise because none of us is wholly good and embody the results of sinful actions and choices in the past by ourselves and others. How in such a situation are we able to act in a way which does not do violence to our moral nature? We have, on the one hand, to act in such a way that we do not imply that the consequences of unmoral acts can be ignored or as treated of no singificance. On the other hand, we have to act in such a way as to bring the greatest good out of the situation and minimize the bad consequences.

To do nothing can represent the abdication of our moral responsibility, even when, as can happen, we do not want to make a decision or to act because we realize the appalling nature of the situation before us. A refusal to act, or a desire to opt out, can because we are so appalled, reflect a profound pessimism about man and lack of confidence in his ability to bring good out of evil. Apart from the inner moral imperative law upon each of us to make a decision, we have also to recognize that for some, especially for those who hold positions of responsibility in government, it is not possible to opt out.

What we have to do is to consider the various courses open to us and to judge that one course, even though it may involve consequences which we would deplore, which we would certainly not describe as good and which we would certainly not intend, is that which we are under a moral obligation to pursue. Our moral nature has been expressed in our assessment of all the courses open and by our acceptance of our obligation to decide and act. I believe we can say that we are fulfilling our moral duty, though we may not be able to say that our actions are wholly morally good.

It is for these reasons that I cannot accept the definition of deterrence in the report of the working party, *The Church and the Bomb*, which reads as follows: 'The ethics of deterrence are the ethics of threatening to do something which one believes would be unmoral, which one intends to do only in circumstances which will not arise because of the conditional threat'.[7] A more accurate and less tendentious definition would be to say that the ethics of deterrence are the ethics of stating the consequences which would follow in certain circumstances, consequences which would be morally right though possibly not morally good, and which it is intended will not arise because the consequences have been made clear.

The distinction which I have drawn is the same as that between the 'right' and the 'good' which dates back to pre-Christian moral philosophers. I have avoided that terminology because, particularly in recent years, the distinction has been increasingly blurred. In popular speech, the 'right' and the 'good' are frequently identified. It is, therefore, better to speak of moral values or ideals, which describe what is good and

moral obligations which describe what is right and what it 1
our duty to do in particular situations.

ULTIMATE SANCTION

When we come to apply these considerations to the issue of
nuclear weapons, we face one particular difficulty. We have to
recognize that there is no system of international law and order
with the means for its enforcement. There can, therefore, be
no mechanism for the review and modification of sanctions by
which law and order is presented and disputes resolved, such
as enabled the abolition of the death penalty in Britain. Whatever local sanctions may, from time to time, be effective in
practice, the *ultimate* sanction for the preservation of peace and
the resolution of disputes lies with the power of nuclear
weapons which will not go away. There is no means by which a
less appalling ultimate sanction can be substituted. Man by his
ingenuity having devised such an ultimate sanction, his moral
nature must be exercised in that context. He must not allow his
own sinfulness to lead him to think that he can dispense with it
and rely upon man's goodwill.

Thielicke has summed up the situation accurately: 'The
question is not whether we will choose between Communism
and world destruction but whether we mean in principle to
acknowledge that in this world might is right . . . If then we decide that might is right we decide against that principle of
order from which the State derives and on which all authority
and law depend'.[8]

It is for this reason that I do not believe that moral man can
abandon the ultimate sanction for law and order nor deliver it
into the hands of those who would have no moral scruples
about its use.

Our moral nature, however, does not simply demand that
we support nuclear deterrence. It and Christian hope requires
us to press for action in other respects. In the first place, it demands detailed consideration of how the deterrent should be
organized and how it should operate. Such consideration involves political and technical factors but they must be taken
into account against the background of the moral requirements
that nuclear weapons should be as selective and accurate as
possible and should by their capability demonstrate that they

are intended for deterrence and not aggression. The demands of morality also require that such consideration takes place and is seen to take place in the context of the intention to prevent war and not to emerge victorious in a conflict in which, as is almost universally agreed, there would be no victors, only losers. An admirable example of the way in which this can be done is to be found in chapter seven by General Sir Hugh Beach.

Secondly, continued attention must be given to the effect of modern technological development, particularly in micro-electronics and communication systems on the use of conventional weapons. Dr Frank Barnaby, nuclear physicist and former head of the Stockholm International Peace Research Institute, has written 'We can now say with confidence that science and technology can provide us with better and better systems for neutralizing tanks and aeroplanes at less cost than existing conventional or nuclear weapon systems. These systems,' he continues, 'can be unambiguously defensive and seen to be defensive by the other side.' Such a development would reduce the danger of nuclear escalation, arising from the existence of battlefield nuclear weapons in Europe and would emphasize the deterrent intention behind the strategic weapons.

Thirdly, if the preservation of peace is to be a major objective, any proposals for reduction or renunciation of nuclear weapons must take place within the context of multilateral negotiations, through which, in the interests of peace, the best positive bargain can be struck.

Our present situation is a judgement upon us all, as individuals, and as nations, demonstrating our rejection of the divine pattern for human life. Our response to that judgement must be a recovery of our moral sense. But this must begin with repentance in every aspect of life, not simply with the repudiation of one result of our sinful condition. We must not allow the results of man's inventiveness and destructiveness to overrule our moral responsibility.

Professor Ulrich Simon, whose father was murdered by the Nazis and whose brother perished in the Soviet Union in the great purges, having reflected on what Scripture says about glory and honour and truth, says 'Without these universals human life is not worth preserving. It may be that we have reached this pass which necessitates the End. Who can pretend that the human race has not already polluted the earth beyond recovery? The innumerable cruelties . . . demand a settling of the account. The delusion of pleasure binds the consumer society and entices the socialist world. Envy reigns. The report does not minimize our sinfulness but it cannot envisage Samson at Gaza. A Milton would have redressed the balance here.'

In the book of Relevation the vision and promise of the eternal peace, in which creation is redeemed and consecrated in Christ, is interwoven with the vision of the defeat of evil and portrayed in all its horror and with which there can be no compromise. The victory of Christ, the Lamb that was slain, has to be implemented to the full before the End of the Ages when the nations will dwell in peace in the City of God.

What does this say to us in our dilemma? I can, like the prophet, only speak as a child stammering for words. We must not simply wait passively for Armageddon. Nor must be seek a peace which is no peace, in which evil could prevail unchallenged and unchecked. I can understand a humanist seeking for a brief respite at whatever cost but as Christians I believe that we can only ask for and work for that fragile peace which is all our sinfulness allows, that peace which deterrence gives, which recognizes evil and seeks to check it while we repent and call others to do the same in the hope that the Lord will give us what is better.

Notes

1. J.A. Baker (ed), *The Church and the Bomb*, London: Hodder & Stoughton, 1982, p. 165
2. R. Harries (ed), *What Hope in an Armed World?* Basingstoke: Pickering & Inglis, 1982, p. 107
3. ibid, p. 88.
4. loc. cit.
5. W. Stein (ed), *Nuclear Weapons and the Christian Conscience*, London: Merlin Press, 1981, p. 12
6. *The Error of Pacifism*, lecture delivered by Gp. Capt. L Cheshire VC at St Lawrence Jewry, 10 January 1979.
7. op. cit. p. 98
8. H. Thielicke, *Theological Ethics* II, London: A & C Black (ET), 1969, p. 481

2
THE INTENTION TO DETER
Gerard Hughes

2. The intention to deter

Whether or not it is immoral to possess nuclear weapons as a deterrent depends on a very large number of considerations. Some, and to my mind some of the most difficult to assess, are such that the philosopher, or the Christian theologian, is unlikely to be in a better position to weigh up the evidence that anyone else. About these it would be simply out of place either to moralize or to claim to speak in the name of the Gospel. To clarify one's mind about which these are is an essential prerequisite for seeing where the more properly moral and theological considerations might bear on the argument. Although this note is about one such properly moral issue, some preliminary ground clearing will be in order.

Some non-moral and non-theological matters are not even in dispute. Such, for example, are that a nuclear war would be a horrendous event; that it probably could not in any meaningful sense be 'won'; that both parties to the arms negotiations would gain many advantages from being able to scale down their nuclear armaments very considerably. None of these truths tell either for or against a policy of deterrence in themselves, despite the way in which anti-deterrent arguments are sometimes presented. The horror of nuclear war is one of the major arguments on which a deterrence policy rests, and the advantages to be gained from a reduction in nuclear weapons, while they do tell in favour of a deterrent at the lowest effective level (whatever that might prove to be) do not tell against the possession of a deterrent altogether.

Other matters are more open for debate. Has the fact that East and West have both had nuclear weapons for the last thirty years in fact prevent nuclear, and even conventional, wars which would otherwise have occurred? This is a matter of historical, not of moral judgement. Would some gesture of unilateral reduction in nuclear weaponry in fact result in a parallel reduction from the other side, and so be an effective first step in the mutual scaling down of the level of deterrence? This is a matter of political judgement, and is as such beyond the competence of moralist or theologian to decide. Is it inevitable that any war whatever between East and West would, given the possession of nuclear weapons, eventually escalate into a nuclear war, and into a war in which strategic nuclear weapons were employed? This is not a question of logic, not even of the 'logic of deterrence'. It requires a political and perhaps a psychological assessment of how governments would react under various kinds of pressure.

I am not, of course, saying that one should not have opinions about any of these questions. In practice one will *have* to form and act upon opinions about them, in the full knowledge that one's opinions, and the policies based on those opinions, might well turn out to be mistaken. My point is rather that the very nature of these issues suggests that anyone who claims to be perfectly clear about them is being either dishonest or naive. And even if it is true (as I believe that it is) that grave moral decisions must be to some extent turn on the answers to these questions, that is not to say that dishonesty or naïvety are any less unfortunate if they appear under the guise of moral insight or Christian commitment.

Nevertheless, it might be urged that the morality of the deterrent simply does not depend *at all* on the complex political, historical, and psychological questions I have just raised. And if that is true, the uncertainty of these matters need not in any way impede the clarity of the moral judgements which can be made about a policy of deterrence. The immorality of a policy of deterrence, it might be argued, can be seen just from a careful analysis of what such a policy entails, quite independently of the political and historical circumstances in which such a policy is to be carried out.

Before we discuss the merits of such a position, it will be well to distinguish it carefully from other positions with which it is easily confused. It is, for instance, quite different from the view that a policy of deterrence is wrong because in fact it will lead inevitably, sooner or later, to a nuclear war. This view depends on a historical assessment. Neither, for the same reason, is it the same as the view that a policy of deterrence is wrong because it simply encourages nations to spend on armaments money that could be far better spent on other things. Finally, it is quite different from the view that some unilateral reduction in armaments is called for as the best way to achieve a more radical multilateral reductiuon. That too is a historical judgement which does nothing to prove that a deterrence policy is somehow wrong in itself. It is this last view alone which I wish to discuss.

"WRONG IN ITSELF"

wrong in itself — as opposed to consequences

The view that an action is wrong in itself is usually contrasted with the view that it is wrong because of the consequences to which it leads. This in turn presupposes that there is some clear way in which we can draw the line between the action in itself and its consequences, so that the action itself can be evaluated independently of those consequences. Can this be done?

Well, it certainly *can* be done. But it is worth seeing exactly what we are doing when we make this distinction, and on what grounds the distinction can be made.

Roughly, the terms we use to describe actions, such as 'lifting one's right arm', 'asking someone to stop', 'singing in the bath', 'disturbing the neighbours', 'signing a contract', 'preventing a war', express the outcome of a selection-process. We have looked at the manifold of human behaviour, and picked out certain aspects of it as being worth labelling because we often need to talk about just those elements in what is going on. Action-words pick out pieces of human behaviour as being of a certain type. Of course, we can do several types of things at once: we can make a contract, make someone happy, and get married just by saying two words. Yet although in saying 'I do' a person might have performed all these actions, making a contract is not the same kind of action as making someone happy, nor is it the same kind of action as getting married. Making a bomb, possessing a deterrent, and preventing a war are by no means one type of action; but it might be the case that what a country does will belong to all three action-types at once.

If we ask whether an action is wrong in itself, a great deal depends on whether we are asking this question about types of action, or about what someone actually did. Asked about types of action, the answer will very often be quite uncontroversial. There is nothing in itself wrong with moving one's finger, nor with firing a gun. But it is in itself wrong to maim another human being, or to start a riot. There is nothing in itself wrong with getting married; and it is in itself wrong to make someone

27

is 'preventing a war' an action? — Is it not the purpose of an action, itself not in the power of the actor, whereas possessing a bomb is in his power.

else unhappy for life. Many of our words for types of action are in our language precisely because the express the moral views we hold – words like 'adultery', 'lying', 'murder' or 'theft'. All these types of action are in themselves wrong, which is tantamount to saying that if one does something which is an instance of just one of those types of action, then what one does will also be wrong.

The trouble is, of course, that very often what a person does is an instance of several types of action; some of these are types of action which are wrong in themselves, and others might very well be not wrong in themselves, or even positively good in themselves. If one then asks of what he has done whether *that* is wrong in itself, the answer is by no means so clear. First of all, we have to decide how to describe what it is that he has done. Our choice here will very often express our moral view – he has broken a promise, he has stopped a riot, he has killed an innocent man. It might be that all three things could have been truly said of what he did. But we will choose a description because of our overall assessment of the morality of what he did. In that case, our description of what he did (the action 'in itself') will be the expression of our moral view; it is not a neutral preliminary to forming that view. Alternatively, precisely in recognizing that all three descriptions of what he did are true, we might find ourselves wondering what to make of an action which is at once a case of promise-breaking, killing an innocent man, and stopping a riot in which hundreds could have been killed. And we might express this complexity by wondering just what was the action 'in itself' that he did, and which other elements in the situation were the consequences of what he did. Was the action in itself just firing a gun – or perhaps even just flexing his finger? Or was the action in itself killing an innocent man, and the prevention of the riot the consequence? Or was the action in itself all of these at once? At this point, the whole terminology of 'actions in themselves' becomes arbitrary. However we decide to resolve it will in itself leave quite untouched the question how the moral dilemma (if we believe there is one) ought to be settled.

We can sum up the discussion so far as follows. If we are talking about types of action, there is often little difficulty in saying which actions are wrong in themselves and which are either neutral or right. But if we are talking about what someone does, the distinction between the action in itself and its consequences will either be an arbitrary one, or else it will express a moral view already arrived at on independent grounds. In neither case can it form the *basis* for a moral assessment.

POSSESSING A DETERRENT

What, then, is to be made of the claim that possessing a deterrent is wrong in itself? I think that the foregoing discussion shows that this claim is either question-begging or else simply unhelpful.

First, let me argue that, understood in one way, it is simply unhelpful. If we ask whether the *type* of action described by the phrase 'possessing a deterrent' is in itself right or wrong, surely the answer is that it is neutral, just as firing a gun is in itself neutral. If all we know about someone was that he possessed a deterrent, we would be unable to pass any moral judgement on what he was about. Merely to know that an action is of that type will be quite unhelpful from the moral point of view. Note that this is not to say that because that type of action is neutral in itself, it follows that every instance of that type of action will likewise be neutral. For clearly, instances of that type of action might well be instances of other types of action as well – for instance, they might be instances of blackmail, or of enforcing a just law, or of discouraging a thief. To say of a type of action that it is neutral in itself leaves every practical moral problem untouched. To solve practical moral problems, one needs not merely to know about the morality of types of action; one needs also to know whether what is being done (or contemplated) really is an instance of that type; one needs to know of what other morally significant types of action it is also an instance; and one needs to have some overall method of assessing actions which instantiate several types at once.

Suppose, then, that one is speaking about a particular case of possessing a nuclear deterrent – say, the present possession of such a deterrent by the Western Powers. Is that possession wrong in itself? I have already shown why this question cannot be solved merely by forming a moral view about the type of action 'possessing a deterrent' in itself, no matter what moral view that might be. Still less can it be solved if one thinks, as I do, that that type of action is in itself morally neutral. To solve the problem, one needs to know what other actions the Western possession of a nuclear deterrent instantiates. Is it, for example, also an instance of preventing a war? Is it an instance of greatly increasing the likelihood of war? If it is an instance just of the first, then this particular possession of a deterrent is surely right. If just of the second, equally surely it is wrong. But to decide which of these is actually the case requires precisely that historical and political judgement to which I referred in the opening section of this paper. At this point, one would have to speak no longer as a moralist or a theologian, but as a historian or a politican. That our moral judgements should thus be at the mercy of other assessments to which as moralists we can make no privileged contribution may possibly seem most unfortunate. But morality is a practical science; and practical science cannot be carried out without actual investigation of the real world. Such investigation is in the very nature of the case complex, to some extent tentative, and open to revision. It is only in the realm of moral theory that the moralist can even aspire to clarity. Aristotle himself warned us against seeking such clarity in the problems of moral practice, and Aquinas echoed his warning. It is still worth taking seriously.

It follows that to assert that possession of the deterrent is in itself immoral will either be to make a theoretical remark (and I believe an implausible one at that) with no practical bearing on the particular instance of the possession of the deterrent by the Western Powers; or else it will be a somewhat misleading way of summarising a lengthy historical and political study – which is why the phrase 'in itself' is out of place. What it cannot be is a claim to have solved a practical moral problem independently of such study. Neither can it be a claim to greater clarity than such study itself permits.

THE INTENTION TO DETER

The argument is not yet finished. It might be objected against what I have said that a crucial element in possessing a deterrent has been fatally ignored. The possession of a deterrent, if it is to be in any way effective, must surely involve the intention to use it if attacked. It must therefore involve the willingness to use nuclear weapons. But given the nature of nuclear weapons, it is surely clear enough that their actual use, whatever might

30

be the case with their mere possession, might be morally wrong. Hence the possession of a deterrent necessarily – 'in itself' one might say – involves forming an intention to do what is morally wrong. One may not morally form such an intention. Hence even possession is 'in itself' morally wrong, despite the preceding argument.

In this paper I shall not discuss whether or not it can be said that any and every use of nuclear weapons is clearly morally wrong. I believe that this is either an unwarranted generalization which ignores the differences between various types of weapon; or else it takes as obvious what I would have thought was a more disputable point, that the use of any nuclear weapon will inevitably lead to the use of any available type of nuclear weapon. Be that as it may, I shall not pause to argue the point here, but shall concede for the sake of the discussion that the actual use of nuclear weapons is wrong. Even so, I do not think that it follows that the possession of a deterrent is necessarily wrong. Let me try to explain why.

One might have thought that the simplest way to meet the point would be to appeal to the morality of bluff. Clearly to bluff successfully one does not necessarily have to intend to do what one bluffingly says one will do. If the bluff is called, one can always give in with a reasonably good grace. I do think that this is a perfectly good theoretical point; and perhaps, since the point about intention is itself usually presented as a theoretical point, this would be an adequate reply. But the case against the deterrent can be presented in a way which is in one respect stronger than the one more usually offered. It might be argued that the point about intention is not a theoretical one; it concerns the actual state of mind which is required of people at this point in history to make this particular instance of the deterrent effective. For the nuclear deterrent as we know it to succeed, it is in practice essential that many of the personnel involved in the chain of command should quite clearly intend to fire their weapons if ordered. It would be in practice impossible for all these people to be merely bluffing without this fact eventually becoming public knowledge. And once it is public knowledge, the deterrent loses much, if not all, of its credibility.

It is worth noting both the strengths and the concessions involved in this way of putting the argument against possession. The strength is that a merely theoretical point about possible bluffs (culled from poker, or *Call my Bluff* or other such harmless activities) will no longer avail against the argument rephrased in this realistic and practical way. This particular bluff is not one which everyone can be willing to have called, whereupon they will give in gracefully. On the other hand, the argument as now rephrased no longer establishes a moral position about the possession of a nuclear deterrent in general – 'in itself', one might say – but rather a conclusion about this particular deterrent, with this particular chain of command, in this particular political setting. But no matter. It is, after all, this particular problem which is the most pressing one.

So it will have to be conceded that the intention involved in possessing a deterrent cannot be merely the intention to bluff, at least not on everyone's part. A political leader might, perhaps, intend no more than bluff. But at the very least, somewhere down the chain of command if not also at the top, there must be people who are not bluffing. If they intend to use nuclear weapons in some circumstance or other, then they do not intend to do something which is (at least for the sake of argument) immoral, and is not this an immoral intention for them to have? Hence is not a system which relies on such intentions itself an immoral one?

This is the only argument known to me which claims to establish that possession of a deterrent is wrong independently of any benefit to peace which the deterrent might produce. But I believe also that it oversimplifies the situation considerably, and that in the end it is not valid. The reply can, I think, take one of two forms.

One can consider the formation of an intention as itself being an action. After all, genuinely to form an intention is not a piece of purely private behaviour, even in the sense in which wishful thinking, for example, might be private. To form an intention will normally be bound up with taking the appropriate steps to put it into practice. As with any other behaviour, then, the question must be asked which types of action does this behaviour instantiate.

The argument we are considering urges that the present possession of a nuclear deterrent by the Western Powers falls under just one morally significant type of action – that of intending to wage nuclear war. However, it is the heart of the case for the deterrent that what the western powers are doing can also be described as preventing nuclear war, or at the very

T as an action
having the intention to prevent.

32

having a *conditional intention* to perform an action...
having as an aim the purpose of avoiding carrying
out the intention.

no. X

least making such a war less likely. Since it is obviously
everyone's duty to prevent nuclear war or to minimize the risk
that one will occur, those in favour of the deterrent would
argue that it is also morally important that this description does
truly describe what is being done.

I have already argued that even if intending to wage nuclear
war is a type of action which could be said to be 'wrong in itself', it by no means follows that every particular action falling
under that description will turn out to be wrong. In the case in
point, the argument in favour of the deterrent points out that
what is being done is not merely intending to wage nuclear
war, but also helping to prevent such a war. We therefore have
a situation in which two moral descriptions, each pointing in
opposite directions, can properly be applied to what is actually
being done. As I remarked, cases involving conflicting moral
descriptions cannot be simply solved. But at least I should have
thought it a reasonable view that the avoidance of nuclear war
was of overriding moral importance. In that case, the possession of the deterrent, even though it involves the intention to
wage nuclear war, is not merely not wrong, it might be argued
to be obligatory.

I think the matter could also be put somewhat differently, to
make the same point. If it is true that the action can properly
be described as preventing nuclear war by taking real preparations for waging one, then the intention of an agent performing
this action is likewise to prevent nuclear war by preparing to
wage it. It is incorrect to express this intention simply as intending to wage nuclear war. It is no doubt paradoxical that
only by maintaining a credible deterrent is it possible to make
nuclear war less likely, and that the more convincing the
preparations the less likely that they will ever be called into
action. But this paradox, if it is one, is not somehow a failure in
the logic of intention, it is a peculiarity of the historical situation in which we are placed. The intentions of well-informed
agents acting in these circumstances will reflect the complexity
of their situation.

There is no logical relationship between the intention to use
the deterrent formed in circumstances where only having that
intention will in fact ensure that it need never be used, and the
intention to use the deterrent in circumstances where it has already failed. In that eventuality, a crucial set of beliefs which
may have led to the formation of the original intention will

ie bluff. You declare as intention which if the
a conditional intention, but if the conditions are
fulfilled, you don't necessarily hold the intention
any more

have been, unfortunately, shown to be false. The agent is no longer committed in logic to take any particular view of the new situation with which he would then be faced. The advocate of the deterrent policy will, believe that only if here and now he fully intends to use it will the deterrent succeed in preventing war. That belief, as I have argued above, will rest on a historical and political judgement which could, of course, turn out to be mistaken. Still, given that he holds that belief, the advocate of the deterrent will certainly say that he fully intends to use nuclear weapons should he be attacked. In so saying he is not, I think, logically committed to give the same answer in the quite different situation which would obtain if he were attacked. In that situation, indeed, it is most unlikely that he would be asked. But until he is asked *in those circumstances*, he need say nothing different from what he will say at the moment.

I conclude, then, that it cannot be shown in any important sense that possession of a deterrent is wrong in itself, or that the advocate of the deterrent is committed to forming an intention which is immoral. The morality of the deterrent cannot be settled just by moral logic. It depends upon a set of highly complex beliefs about the results of the various policies we could adopt. I see nothing in moral theory which justifies the attempt to short-circuit these practical problems, or to claim greater clarity in the nuclear debate than our uncertain beliefs in these areas will warrant.

3
THE MORAL CONFUSION OF UNILATERALISM
Francis Bridger

the risk is that we declare an
intentions in order to prevent
being fulfilled.

If the intention is fulfilled the purpose
is thereby lost. There is no
holding & carrying out the
intention may therefore be
cancelled.

Presumably we have the possibility in
advance, therefore know that we
will withdraw intention if the
condition is fulfilled.

We said we would ... intention would be
cancelled if ... fulfilled.

That we said we are the purpose which
was to carry out what we said if
it didn't fulfil its purpose.

Therefore the argumentation
behind a policy (that) not of genuine
nuclear deterrence, — we know in
advance we will not carry out our
and intention even if the intention is
fulfilled.

3. The moral confusion of unilateralism

For the morally-sensitive Christian trying to thread his way through the nuclear maze, the complexity of the issue seems at times overwhelming. In consequence, two stereotypes beckon with great appeal. The first is that of the unilateralist whose case appears morally superior (and is presented as such), not least because of unilateralism's self-styled designation as 'the peace movement'. The second is that of the multilateralist, who is frequently portrayed as at worst a warmonger, at best an insensitive worldly-wise cynic who fails to think at all in moral categories. Anyone who has seen some of the anti-nuclear propaganda will recognize the force of these stereotypes.

The difficulty is compounded by three further factors. Firstly, the unilateralist case is frequently – if not invariably – presented as morally self-evident: nuclear weapons are intrinsically and obviously immoral, and the strategy of deterrence indefensible. No right-thinking moral person could conceivably have anything to do with them.

Secondly, the skilful and vocal capturing of media and public attention by CND, coupled with its flair for the dramatic demonstration, has meant that the agenda has effectively been set by the moral dictates of unilateralism. The individual endeavouring to reason his way through the issues is met with the relentless pressure of unilateralist presuppositions. Faced with a self-validating moral stance, righteously proclaimed, the inquirer perceives a new orthodoxy which he may well be hesitant to challenge. Even though he may not be convinced rationally, on an emotive level the pull towards unilateralism is strong.

Thirdly, there is a profound appeal in the simplicity of the CND case, particularly in its Christian manifestation. It chimes with a thoughtful Christian's view of creation, the incarnation, and the kingship of God. Moreover, its claim to be the movement of peace, its renunciation of weapons which by any definition are horrific, and its implicit claim somehow

37

to be 'more loving' evoke the deepest feelings of any morally-conscious person.

Over and against this, the proponent of deterrence faces a double problem: it is relatively easy to construct a case for unilateral disarmament, to give it *prima facie* moral justification, and to sell it to a fearful public opinion. The phrase 'protest and survive' is a testimony to the power of the simplistic slogan which strikes chords with deepest human fears. But it is much more difficult to present the complex moral case for deterrence in a few swift sentences. For the case does involve some careful reasoning and a respect for the complexity of the question. It also, for many Christians at least, involves an unwelcome encounter with political reality, the nature of States, and their behaviour. The character of international relations stands in unpleasant contrast to the 'Kingdom utopianism' which permeates the discussion of the issue by some Western theological writers.

It is important, however, to realize that behind the apparent simplicity of unilateralist moralism, there lie major ambiguities and contradictions which seriously undermine the strength of its case. This essay will focus upon two such areas.

1. INTRINSIC VERSUS CONSEQUENTIAL ETHICS

Gerry Hughes in the previous chapter has shown the difficulty of viewing moral acts as wrong in themselves independent of consequences. Yet this assumption dominates much (though not all) Christian unilateralism. *The Church and the Bomb*, although equivocal at times, speaks of nuclear weapons as being 'in absolute contradiction' to the concept of peace. Deterrence is unacceptable for 'Even the possession and possible conditional intention to use nuclear weapons is itself immoral'. There are 'huge moral imperatives against using nuclear weapons at all'.[1] The report, moreover, endorses an 'approach to moral thinking which presupposes that there is a class of actions which are intrinsically evil . . . If an action belongs to that class no intention, however good, and no circumstances can justify it'. Given the conclusions of the report, it seems obvious that current nuclear strategies and policies, especially deterrence, fall within this category.[2]

This intrinsic moral absolutism is typical of Christian unilateralism across the denominational spectrum. John Stott, a leading British Anglican Evangelical has argued that

'. . . it seems clear to me that (nuclear weapons) are ethically indefensible, and that every Christian . . . must be a nuclear pacifist'.[3]

Similarly the Sojourners group in the USA:

'Our primary allegiance to Jesus Christ and His Kingdom commits us to total abolition of nuclear weapons. There can be no qualifying or conditioning word.'[4]

Alan Kreider, Director of the London Mennonite Centre, has declared:

'As Christians we can never stop with analysing the effectiveness of a policy. We must also assess its faithfulness to God's will as revealed in Scripture. And by this standard as well, the policies undergirding the arms race are misguided. Not only are they not working; they are wrong.'

Moreover,

'in view of the dictates of Christian morality, (British policy) must go further, to the rejection by the UK of all nuclear weapons, and the withdrawal of British facilities to American nuclear forces.'[5]

The Religious Society of Friends is unequivocal:

'We feel bound explicitly to avow our unshaken persuasion that all war is utterly incompatible with plain precepts of our divine Lord and Lawgiver, and the whole spirit of His Gospel, and that no plea of necessity or policy, however urgent or peculiar, can avail to release either individuals or nations from the paramount allegiance which they owe to Him who has said "Love your enemies".'[6]

On the Roman Catholic side, Bishop Roger Mahony, bishop of Stockton, California, has urged that

'. . . a form of nuclear pacifism is a weighty and unexceptional obligation of Christians . . . No Catholic can ever support or cooperate with the planning or executing of policies to use, or which by implication intend to use, nuclear weapons even in a defensive posture . . .'[7]

Mgr Bruce Kent has written off non-unilateralist Christians sweepingly:

'The Society of Friends apart, how little they (the churches) have so far done and how tied they are to national prejudices, how wedded to a moral theology of war that makes counting angels on the tips of needles sound by comparison a most constructive pastime.'[8]

The undecided Christian is thus confronted with an overwhelming consensus – nuclear weapons *per se*, and the possession of them even for purely deterrent purposes, are condemned. No Christian can properly accept their retention.

Upon closer inspection, however, it becomes clear that this position is open to serious challenge. As Gerry Hughes has shown, the distinction between 'wrong in itself' and 'wrong because of certain consequences' is by no means as clear cut as has been argued. But even if we do accept such a distinction and argue within its own terms, we still discover a series of ambiguities and contradictions.

The clearest example of this lies in *The Church and the Bomb,* and in subsequent pronouncements by its authors. Having endorsed, as we have seen, an intrinsicalist ethic, the report nevertheless tries to ride the consequentialist horse at the same time. The possession of nuclear arms, the logic of deterrence, the possible conditional intent to use them, are all dismissed on the grounds that they are in themselves immoral. Even if, for argument's sake, such weapons do keep the peace, it is still wrong to rely on them since such reliance depends on acting immorally. It is not acceptable to do evil that good may come.

This seems clear enough. The final recommendations of the report, however, are couched in consequentialist terms. Unilateral British renunciation is proposed because 'there is a need for new disarmament strategies . . . which will break the logjam in which we seem to be caught'. Moreover, Paul

Oestreicher, one of the authors, in a letter to *The Times* on 11 December 1982 denied that consequences could be ignored:

'Would we maintain our qualified unilateralism were we persuaded that this would make nuclear war more likely? Of course not. But we are not so persuaded.'

The unilateralist argument becomes even more confused in the light of an article in May 1983 by the Bishop of Salisbury, chairman of the working party which produced *The Church and the Bomb*. In a crucial passage he wrote:

'We need to reduce the number of nuclear weapons in the world. We could start now, cutting down our own weapons independently, without any risk whatsoever, whether the Soviet Union reciprocate or not. *All we have to do is to keep enough submarines to deter.*'

It is difficult to see how this can be squared with the conclusions of the report which reject the notion of deterrence and call for immediate renunciation by Britain of nuclear capabilities. However, the central point in relation to the report, Paul Oestreicher's letter, and the Bishop's article is that they are all thoroughly consequentialist in their reasoning, despite their earlier avowal of 'an approach to moral thinking which presupposes that there is a class of actions which are intrinsically evil'.

Within the terms of their own argument, this cannot be sustained. The appeal to consequences cannot properly be made from an intrinsicalist standpoint. If it is wrong to have nuclear weapons *per se*, then they must be renounced, irrespective of consequences. The justification for renunciation likewise cannot be made by appeal to the importance of breaking log-jams and so on. They must be disposed of simply because they are in themselves evil, not because we believe their renunciation will have certain consequences. This major contradiction cannot be overlooked, and will give the questioning inquirer pause for thought about the coherence of the unilateralist case.

2. WEST AND EAST

A second area of moral confusion lies in the frequent assumption that there exists a rough moral equivalence between Soviet

41

and Western social systems. Chapter four of *The Church and the Bomb* typifies this type of reasoning well. By a selection process which is unexplained and arbitrary, the history of East-West relations since 1945 is interpreted and portrayed in such a way as to suggest that both are as bad (or as good) as each other. The ideological confrontation is not viewed in moral terms, or in terms of evaluating one against the other, but essentially as no more than a conflicting power struggle.[10] The discussion is thoroughly relativistic: there is a complete absence of any attempt to weigh either system against Christian or any other, morality. Interestingly, the 'vicious brutality' of the CIA is condemned without discussion[11] but the reader will search in vain to find any mention at all of the KGB or its Eastern European counterparts.

All this is not to suggest that the West has an unblemished record, or that Western societies will not also one day sit under the judgement of God. What is significant, however, from the moral point of view, is that a relativist attitude towards the Soviet system can by a short route lead to the belief that Western democracies are not worth defending, or that the Soviet state is not so bad after all.

But despite the revisionist approach of *The Church and the Bomb*, these conclusions must be resisted. The democracies, for all their failings (to which no one can be blind), embody values which lie closer to the Christian vision than does Soviet totalitarianism. The attempt to control every area of individual and corporate life, the refusal of political choice, the use of violence and terror for social and political ends, the deliberate construction of the apparatus of a police state, the abuse of psychiatry for penal purposes, the establishment of labour camps, the crushing of dissidents, the persecution of Jews and other religious believers, the literal fencing-in of its citizens so that few can choose to live under a free system, the imposition of similar structures on neighbouring countries – all these are characteristic features of the Soviet system which are conspicuously absent from the West.

This point has been made with great force by Alexander Solzhenitsyn. Commenting on the notion of submission to Soviet control as morally superior, he has argued that:

'I shall only say about the famous axiom "Better to be red than dead" that there is no alternative in it because to become red is really in fact to die a slow death. The free people of the West have missed sixty-five years. They have stood there fully armed and not struggled. When they give in to communism they will find themselves as slaves, and what is more moribund slaves. That's when they will begin to fight but in different conditions. And what is so amazing is that the West appears not to hear the absolutely explicit condemnation to death which has been pronounced. In 1919, the Comintern was created and its leaders, Lenin and Trotsky, who at that point had absolutely no nuclear arms, they hardly had any rifles or bullets to put into them, but none the less they declared a condemnation to death for the Western world; and the West laughed. Sixty years ago, the whole of educated Russia, the cream of Russian intellectual development, the whole intelligentsia, *everybody*, said "look, this is something quite unlike anything you have seen before", the West turned a totally deaf ear. Fifty years ago the logs of wood from the camps with things written in the blood of those who were imprisoned up in the north, those logs of wood somehow came to the West. Forty years ago millions of Soviet people again told of the horrors. They were not only not listened to but in their hundreds of thousands and millions were simply given back and betrayed to captivity and certain death in the Soviet Union. Thirty years ago, Kravchenko in the famous trial hearing in Paris revealed the true nature of the Soviet regime and he wasn't listened to, either. History does not forgive such multiple mistakes.'[12]

When *The Church and the Bomb* therefore speaks with studied evenhandedness about East and West, it is propounding a flawed and insensitive morality. The respective systems are blatantly not equivalent, and when the tone of the report suggests otherwise its authors should be aware that they are free to do so only because this equivalence is lacking.

What can be positively said from the standpoint of moral theology about Western democracies? In his book *The Children of Light and the Children of Darkness* (1945), Reinhold Niebuhr set out theologically to provide 'a vindication of democracy and a critique of its traditional defenders'.[13] Space does not allow more than a charting of his key points, but they are significant in our present discussion of Western values.

43

Niebuhr's central argument is that although liberal humanistic democracy is wrong-footed in its optimistic view of man's ability to achieve an easy resolution of the tension between self-interest and the general interest, it nevertheless offers the best conditions for the development of that moral responsibility and creativity which are the hallmarks of God's image in man. This requires not simply subjective, inner freedom of thought and feelings, but objective conditions which enable free relationships to develop, and in which men can freely and creatively make decisions for the ordering of their lives individually and corporately. This tension between liberty and community is reflected in the ambiguities of democracy, but it is precluded by totalitarianism. Thus, Niebuhr declares, 'a free society is justified by the fact that the indeterminate possibilities of human vitality may be creative'.[14]

Our assessment of Western values will therefore inevitably come back to our doctrine of man. He is made in the image of God with creativity and freedom, but he is flawed. The Fall has not destroyed the divine image in men, but it has marred it. Consequently human life is highly ambiguous. In the redemptive plan of God, these contradictions will ultimately be resolved. But until that eschatological fulfilment, our social organization must recognize the tension between what God would have us to be and what we, as men, actually are. Western democracy with its understanding of the need for checks and balances of power represents a better approximation (however rough) to Christian realism than does Soviet totalitarianism. In Niebuhr's words again, 'Man's capacity for justice makes democracy possible; but man's inclination to injustice makes democracy necessary'.[15]

It can be seen, therefore, that the equation between East and West is inadequate, shallow and morally confused. It is a tragic paradox that much unilaterist argument depends for its very existence and expression upon a system which it finds hard morally to distinguish from its Eastern alternative. Moreover, even if submission were to mean the condemnation of millions to the labour camp, the Gulag, and the torture chamber, this would somehow be regarded as acceptable. It is thus an ironic paradox that those who advocate a strategy of deterrence as a way of preserving freedom, dignity and peace are somehow regarded as less moral.

Notes

1. J. A. Baker (ed.), *The Church and the Bomb*, London: Hodder & Stoughton, 1982, p. 154.
2. op cit. pp. 99–100
3. J. Stott 'Calling for Peacemakers in a Nuclear Age' in *Christianity Today*, 7 March 1980, p. 45.
4. J. C. Grannis, A. J. Laffin & E. Schade (eds), *The Risk of the Cross*, NY: Seabury Press, 1981, p. 80. See also *The Sojourner*, August 1981, *passim*
5. J. Stott (Ed), *The Year AD 2000*, Basingstoke: Marshall, Morgan & Scott, 1983, pp. 35, 44.
6. J.C. Grannis, op. cit. p. 80
7. E. W. Lefever & E. S. Hunt (eds), *The Apocalyptic Premise*, Washington DC: Ethics & Public Policy Center, 1982, p. 282
8. E. P. Thompson & Dan Smith (Eds), *Protest & Survive*, London: Penguin 1980, p. 255.
9. *Church of England Newspaper*, 20 May 1983, p. 5.
10. 'Politically, the rivalry between the Soviet Union and the United States is a classic struggle between two great powers, both of whom . . . seek to deny the character of the struggle,' *The Church and the Bomb*, p. 67. On this basis all moral categories are reduced to power politics. This is an entirely reductionist approach.
11. op.cit. p. 72.
12. *The Times*, 23 May 1983, p. 11.
13. Reinhold Niebuhr, *The Children of Light and the Children of Darkness* London: Nisbet & Co, 1945, title page.
14. ibid. p. 48
15. ibid. p. vi

4
THE JUST WAR AND NUCLEAR ARMS

Keith Ward

4. The just war and nuclear arms

There are over 14,500 recorded wars in the known history of the human race. According to the Brookings Institute, there have been 127 wars in the world since the end of the Second World War, in which an estimated 32 million people have been killed or wounded. Even as I write, people are being killed in conflicts in Iran, Afghanistan, Ethiopia, El Salvador, and even within the United Kingdom. It is, regrettably, completely false to say that all the peoples of the world want peace. If they do want peace, it is very much on their own terms; and they are evidently prepared to resort to armed conflict to get the terms they want – whether in territory, control of material resources or the establishment of a particular conception of justice. Thus violent conflict is part of the normal condition of human kind. I do not praise this fact or approve of it. But it is a fact, from which we must begin, that people do frequently seek to impose their will on others, to repress and kill them, to destroy their cultures and annex their territories by extreme and violent means.

The first moral question we must face is how we should act in a world like this. If a great evil is being done, great suffering being caused; if it is being done to people for whom we are responsible, our kinfolk, fellow citizens, our families and children; how should we react? That is the problem with which the meanstream tradition of Christian thinking about war begins.

Christian ethics is a continuing attempt to measure the absolute ethics of the kingdom against the harsh realities of a world corrupted by evil. Of course, we know that as Christians, as human beings, we are called to strive for increased knowledge, understanding and sensitivity; greater creativity and originality; wiser love for, delight in and care for others. Of course, we are called to seek peace; that positive peace which lies in positive co-operation in pursuit of freely chosen purposes, and enjoyment of the diversity of human aims and characters. We are called to worship God and enjoy him for ever. We know these things without doubt, even if we need to keep reminding ourselves of them, in the midst of the pressing routines of everyday life.

Because we know these things so clearly, it may be felt that we should never knowingly do anything to cause harm or frustrate peace; that we should always, in every circumstance, refrain from doing evil. This is the stance of moral absolutism. It entails that, if killing is wrong, then I should never kill, whatever the circumstances. If someone threatens me with violence, then at least I cannot offer violence in return. It entails a policy of submission to evil.

There have always been some Christians who have adopted this position – probably inspired in the main by a certain interpretation of the crucifixion as the submission of God himself to evil. However, it has been rejected by the mainstream Christian traditions, who have perhaps emphasized that Christ is the judge of all the world. His crucifixion, on the mainstream view, is not a passive submission to evil, but a freely accepted sharing in the suffering of humanity, which is not seen properly unless one sees also the resurrection and the coming in judgement, the triumph of goodness by the final extermination of evil for ever. Evil will be conquered by the power of God; and that God is the same Lord of Hosts who was with the people of Israel in battle, and who delivered them from Egypt by drowning the Egyptian host. I think it does little justice to the biblical God to see him as simply submitting to evil on the cross, letting it conquer. That sort of passive goodness does not conquer. What conquers evil is the return on the clouds of glory, asserting the power which had only been restrained, but not given up, at Calvary. God does not submit to evil. He shares in its consequences; but he cannot be conquered by death; and he will come again to extirpate it from his creation, by the swords of his angelic armies.

Naturally, much of this language is poetic or metaphorical. But it is, I think, a perverse view of the Biblical tradition which sees it as encouraging passive resistance to evil. The God who led the Israelites into battle; who will judge the world in the person of Jesus; whose power is unlimited and whose holiness is absolute – that God is not one who just lets evil and destruction finally rule in his creation.

It is a contemporary cultural phenomenon in Britain that we sometimes see God as sympathetically shrugging his shoulders over sin; and that we see 'love' as primarily a two-person, intensely sympathetic and deeply committed phenomenon. So, like our God, we sympathetically shrug our shoulders when the person we are 'loving' does something terribly evil. To understand all is to forgive all; and we are even prepared to think that the evil may be partly due to our lack of understanding. We do not face the problem of what love should do when it is faced by something evil; of what love should do when it is extended to a group of people who are causing great harm to each other; of what love can be in a world like this.

It seems to me clear that love must be concern for the well-being of other persons. And that does not mean letting them do whatever they like. To see people systematically destroying themselves, and do nothing about it, does not seem to show real concern for their flourishing. In a Christian perspective, the well-being of persons must consist of their growth in understanding, individuality and sympathy; in a deepening concern for truth, beauty and goodness. And it must consist in learning to love and obey God. Suppose that we wish to further these things in someone else; and suppose we see them becoming deceitful, slovenly and resentful. What should we do? Should we not show our concern by unmistakably condemning their course? By anger and opposition? By expressing outrage and the strongest disapproval?

Outrage without any strong underlying sympathy will only alienate. Sympathy without any anger at wrong-doing will only undermine respect. It is essential that love should exist; and equally essential that it should not always be soft, self-giving and too readily forgiving. By that, I do not mean that forgiveness should not be freely offered; of course it should, 'seventy times seven' times. But only on the condition of repentance and, if possible, restitution or at least amendment. The sort of forgiveness which is wrong is that which is so easily given that the wrong-doing is taken not to have mattered; that which costs nothing, either to the forgiver or to the wrong-doer. It is a terrible theological mistake to say that God's forgiveness is unconditional. It is not. It has very definite and difficult conditions – repentance and faith. And who knows the cost and the depth of those?

My case is that wrong-doing must be opposed, out of respect and concern for the wrong-doers as well as for any who may be influenced by them. And that may well mean the use of force. So love itself may require violence. The parents who never discipline their children are not truly caring for them, or for what they may become. Now of course there are different ways of discipline. I am not suggesting that parents should kill or maim very naughty children (though see Deuteronomy 21). Non-physical punishments may be very preferable to physical ones; and one must certainly guard against the possibility of vindictiveness or sadism. I am only arguing for the principle that it is sometimes right to cause harm to another human being. For we must be clear-headed enough to see that discipline of another is a sort of harm; it is doing something which causes them pain, against their will. It is in vain to argue that 'it is for their own good, in the long run'. The fact is that, in punishment, we are causing harm to someone, in the hope and with the final intention that it will promote their good. But whether it does or not depends upon their response. The good is not within our power; the harm is. Thus it is that love can lead us to harm someone – namely, when they are committed to a course of self-destructive evil. The harm we cause, we say, is less than the harm they will otherwise ultimately bring on themselves. And so we come to the ethical principle which is of fundamental importance for the theory of the 'Just War' – it is permissible, at least in some circumstances, to commit an evil act (one causing harm) in order to prevent a much greater evil, when there is no other way of preventing that greater evil. In the cases under consideration, we cause harm simply *in the hope* of preventing the greater evil. We cannot guarantee it, since it depends on the choices of other people.

If this is so, with regard to one person for whom we have some responsibility and over whom we have some legitimate authority (for I am not suggesting that anyone can go around harming other people who are thought to be evil, without responsibility or authority), it is much more so when we see one person causing harm to others. Suppose that we are trying to love two people impartially, and one of them decides to torture the other to death. How then may love be exercised? If we do nothing, one person will die in agony. If we manage to wound and disable the torturer, we will have directly harmed someone. But an innocent person will go free; and the aggressor will only have himself to blame for his injuries.

There are three relevant factors in the case. First, with regard to the amount, intensity and duration of harm, I must obviously wade into the attack; since it will be much less if I

50

do. Second, there is the matter of the punishment of aggression; the fact that it should be prevented, and that it should not be seen to pay. Together with this is the principle that the innocent should be protected from harm. On this count, I should clearly attack; for only so can the innocent be protected and the aggressor prevented or punished. Thirdly, there is the question of whether I should personally commit evil, by wounding and disabling someone. For the sort of moral absolutist I have mentioned, the answer would be 'no'; and this would outweigh both other factors.

ACTS AND OMISSIONS

Such an absolutist must maintain some form of what is called the 'Acts and Omissions' doctrine. This doctrine holds that there is a fundamental moral distinction between doing something and refraining from doing something, even if the consequences are the same. If I push you in the river and you drown, that is much worse than if I see you fall and drown, and do nothing about it, even though I could easily have jumped in and saved you, and I was the only person there. Similarly, if I kill a baby by injecting it with a fatal drug, that is worse than letting it die without feeding it. Both things are indisputably evil (in default of some further explanation); but the positive action is worse.

That may be so. But suppose, now, that the consequences of not acting are much worse than the consequences of positive action. I can kill the baby immediately and painlessly; or let it die in a slow agony. I push you under the water; or I watch you for half an hour, vainly struggling to get out. Given that both are still wrong, is it still clear that it is worse to act positively, and get the thing over with? We may hesitate, because there may be a third way; someone may come along and save you, if I have not actually killed you. The positive act seems worse, perhaps, because it is so final. To eliminate this complication, suppose that I have to do one of these things; there is no possible alternative – I either have to push you under, or leave you to drown slowly. In that case, would it not be worse to prolong your agony? Well, yes; but only if you let the consequences outweigh an absolute prohibition on killing, you may say.

51

To estimate the force of this reply, consider another, much more extreme (but not impossible) case. During a war, the enemy lines up thirty women and children, and says that he will shoot them, unless I myself shoot the one person I alone know to be responsible for a previous sabotage attack. I refuse, and he begins to shoot the women; so I know there is no bluff. What should I do? Is it better to permit so much evil than to shoot one man? If I am under an absolute obligation not to kill, am I not also under an absolute obligation not to permit preventable evil? I cannot escape by saying that the evil is his responsibility. It is; but since I could stop it, it is also mine. I can only prevent evil by doing evil; and since, the evil I would prevent is undoubtedly greater than the evil I do, considered impartially, all the emphasis must fall on the fact that I am doing it.

It seems to me that this is a clear case of a genuine moral dilemma. I have an obligation, in general, not to kill. But I also have an obligation, in general, to prevent evil, if I can do so fairly easily and no-one else can. These obligations conflict; and what is not clear, is which should take precedence. I must necessarily fail to carry out one of these obligations; there is no escape. Further, I think it is implausible to hold that it is always worse to commit an evil, however small, than to fail to do good, however great and necessary. Telling a harmless lie, for example, seems clearly better than failing to save a life.

These two points, though they may seem rather remote from the subject of nuclear deterrence, are in fact quite central to it. Very often, people simply have not thought their moral principles through far enough, to see what they are, at the most basic level. My suggestion, prompted by these simple examples, is that there do occur real moral dilemmas. That is, there are conflicts of duty, where you cannot avoid doing something that is, in general, wrong. You cannot be, strictly speaking, guilty for such breaches of duty, since they are inevitable, whatever you do. But they will cause unease; they are, in the real sense, tragic. For, in these cases, there is no possibility of avoiding evil.

In the case of nuclear deterrence, there is just such a moral dilemma; indeed, just about the worst one conceivable. The dilemma is that, on the one hand, you ought not to threaten, or seem to threaten, however conditionally, to destroy millions of innocent people by massive nuclear attack. But, on the other hand, you ought not to allow a tyrannical and oppressive regime to attack and conquer your country, if you have a means of preventing it. If this is right – and I will defend it in a moment – then, whatever you do will be in breach of some great duty. I think it is important to stress this, for there are absolutists who hold that real dilemmas never occur, and that it is always possible not to do evil, whatever the consequences. In this world, on the contrary, there are times when one has to do something evil, to prevent a greater evil. There is no choice. Whichever way we choose, we are doing evil to prevent evil. The only possible reply to this would be to say that permitting a great and avoidable evil was not a case of 'doing evil'. That would, I think, be word-play of the worst sort. For permitting evil is wrong, if it is avoidable; therefore such permitting is a form of doing wrong, even if it just consists of sitting still. Doing wrong is clearly doing evil; so the conclusion is unavoidable that permitting avoidable evil is in fact doing something evil. It is choosing to refrain rather to act positively; and voluntary self-restraint is a form of action.

UNAVOIDABLE EVIL

So the first point is that, in this world, it is not possible to avoid doing evil. Clearly, then, we must do the least of the available evils. And this is where the second point comes in. This is, that where duties conflict, we cannot always decide what we should do simply by ruling in advance that a positive act is always worse than an omission. I have mentioned a number of rather difficult cases. Let me put an easier one. If a man runs amok with a machine-gun in a supermarket, and the only way to stop him killing everyone in sight is to shoot him, and if you had a gun, what would you do? It does seem to me clear that we ought to shoot him. This will prevent a much greater amount of harm in suffering and death. It will protect the innocent and prevent the evil of aggression. And the wrong I do by killing one person is much less than the wrong I do by permitting many people to be killed by an aggressor, when I could stop it easily.

I think that the only reason one may still feel a reservation here is that, if you once justify acts of killing, in order to prevent greater evils, that justification may be abused too easily. It may be better to rule out killing absolutely (even in cases where it would prevent greater harm) because such a prohibition will prevent much more harm, overall. The argument is similar to that used for not arming the British police. Although it may be better, in particular cases, for them to be armed, in general it is better that they are not – for then, criminals will not arm themselves; there will be fewer accidental killings; and there will be a lower general level of violent crime.

That is a very strong argument. But, as we have unfortunately seen in Britain in recent years, it will only hold so long as it is true that criminals are not armed and violent. One will need continually to re-assess the situation, and ask whether a total prohibition is achieving its ends – of lowering the general level of violent crime – or not. If circumstances change, then at least some police will need to be armed – and this is in fact what has happened in recent years. Thus an absolute prohibition on killing is only justifiable so long as it does achieve its ends – of decreasing harm in general.

In a very violent world, it would be wrong to prohibit killing absolutely. But it would be right to try to minimize violence, both by restricting the numbers of people who may legitimately be the instruments and the objects of violence, and by placing limits on the kind or degree of violence that may be offered. These are the basic principles which underlie the 'Just War' doctrine. That doctrine is not uniquely a Christian doctrine, but it has developed largely within the Christian tradition as theologians sought to work out how impartial love could be exercised in a world of violence. Their basic conclusion, as expressed by Vitoria, was 'there is a single and only just cause for commencing a war . . . namely, a wrong received'. War is not a matter of killing by private individuals. A war is carried on by specially trained forces; it is commanded by a sovereign authority; and its conduct is, or may be, limited by conventions of various sorts, as agreed between the warring powers. Thomas Aquinas stated that a war must be declared by a legitimate sovereign, for a just cause, and it must be waged by just means. A 'just war' is one which meets these requirements. It is not, and has never been thought to be, a positively good thing. It is a use of well-regulated but violent force, a commission of evil, in order to prevent a greater evil.

What is that greater evil? It is, Vitoria said, 'A wrong received'. Or, of course, it may be a wrong threatened, which can only be prevented by armed opposition. Such a wrong must be a gross injustice, an assault upon the rights of a people. The most basic human rights were defined by John Locke, and embodied in the American Constitution, as the rights to 'life, liberty and estates' – to secure existence, freedom from slavery or oppression, political independence, equality before the law, freedom of thought, belief, religion and association, and security within the borders of one's own legitimate territory. The infringement, or threat of infringement, of these rights constitutes 'a wrong received', and a cause for armed resistance.

It is important to see that what is at stake is justice; not some simple counting of people likely to be killed. That is, we cannot say, 'We will only oppose invasion if more people are likely to be killed if we do not'. All invaders come in peace; there is nothing they want more than peaceful surrender. And, very often, more lives will be lost in opposition than would be lost by such surrender. The Second World War cost 50 million lives. Who can say that is less than surrender to the Axis powers would have cost? But that is not the point. We do not just have to count heads, to decide on the 'greater evil'. We have to try to assess the cost in terms of human repression, exploitation and victimization. And we have to bear in mind that aggression itself is an injustice, which should be prevented if at all possible.

There is another factor, too. We have special responsibilities based upon ties of affection, loyalty, family and kinship, which lay upon us special duties to some people that we do not have to others. We may talk, rather glibly at times, about 'love for all people'. But unless that is spelled out in particular relationships, it is likely to be vacuous and self-deluding – one who tries to love everyone equally will love no-one adequately. So most people would protect their own families, parents and children, at almost any cost. They will feel that they have responsibilities to their own children that they do not have to other people's. They will feel a special concern for the survival of their own culture, language and traditions that they do not feel for others. Naturally, you must admit the right and duty of others to care for their families and cultures too. But you do not have the same responsibility for that as you do for your own family, community and country.

I am not suggesting an insular attitude, or one which says, 'My family (or country) right or wrong', and certainly not one which fosters active dislike or contempt for others. I am simply pointing out the fact that if your responsibilities are not particular, they will be vacuous. We need to cultivate love in particular ways, by taking on specific responsibilities for the groups of people with which we are associated. Thus we have a duty to defend our families and cultures, our communities and countries from destruction, tyranny and subjugation, if we can do so.

There will certainly be a complication if we consider that our country is itself radically unjust. Even then, however, I would not say that we have no duty to obey the sovereign authority (by paying taxes, obeying the laws and so on). Instead, we have another moral dilemma – our duty of obeying the legitimate authority is in opposition to our duty of striving to eliminate injustice. I do not, however, wish to explore that dilemma here. The North Atlantic Treaty of 4 April 1949, states: 'The Parties to this Treaty . . . are determined to safeguard the freedom, common heritage and civilization of their peoples, founded on the principles of democracy, individual liberty and the rule of law'. If those are the values which define our idea of justice; and if that is the ultimate sovereignty (NATO) which, with the free consent of our national government, is responsible for our defence against aggression; then there is no such dilemma there. We have an unqualified duty to support the North Atlantic Treaty defensive alliance and the just societies which it seeks to preserve.

Appeal to the 'Just War' tradition suggests, then, that a defensive resort to armed violence would be justified in order to repel or prevent armed aggression, threatening the fundamental rights of people for whom we have special responsibility. Even so, there will be some limits we may wish to place on the waging of such a 'justifiable' war. These limits have been formulated, within the tradition, as the principles of discrimination and proportion. Both these principles have been formulated in many different ways; and it is difficult to make them precise and comprehensive. But, in some sense, almost all just war theorists have wanted to accept them. They are of special relevance to the issue of nuclear deterrence; since it is because nuclear war is understood to contravene these principles that it is sometimes called immoral in principle. We must therefore examine them quite carefully.

The principle of discrimination attempts to limit the number of people who may be the objects of violence in war. Force must be used with discrimination; it must be the minimum necessary; it must tend materially to the end of victory; and it should not involve the killing of the innocent. These points are enshrined in the Geneva and Hague conventions. They are part of the 'law of war'; and it is clear that anything which limits conflict in this way is better than allowing total war, in which absolutely anything is permitted. Nevertheless, however important they are, these are still conventions. They may be overruled in supreme emergency.

Just as there are absolutists in favour of not killing at all; so there are absolutists in favour of never killing the innocent – those who say that killing the innocent cannot be justified in any circumstances. But the truth seems to be the same in the one case as in the other – killing the innocent can be justified, if it is unavoidably necessary to prevent a greater harm. The point is not often put as bluntly as this, and for good reason. The reason is that, once we license killing the innocent, there seems to be no moral objection to acts of gross terrorism, to a complete breakdown of human rights and to indiscriminate killing to achieve almost any end thought to be worth achieving. We are rightly reluctant to start on that path.

Certainly, killing an innocent person is worse than killing someone who is attacking you. An aggressor may be taken to have forfeited his right to life, by his own action, whereas an innocent person's rights remain intact. It does seem rather odd to defend human rights by contravening them. It is the existence of the right to life which prevents us from simply killing people (for instance, rich old misers) just to increase the general happiness. The preservation of that right is of extreme importance; and that is why we are reluctant to justify violating it, even to prevent greater harm. Since the preservation of human rights does decrease harm in general, it will be wrong to violate them in particular cases, even when such violation will decrease harm. We have to weigh the harm caused by the violation of a fundamental right against the harm caused by letting the feared evil occur. It will be extremely rare for the particular harm to outweigh the general harm of a breakdown of human rights; so rare that the principle of not killing the innocent is almost inviolable.

Almost, but not quite. There comes a point at which even the violation of the right to life is less wrong than some other evil, which cannot otherwise be avoided. This point cannot be determined by a purely utilitarian calculation, for it is not just different quantities of the same thing (happiness) which are being weighed against one another; it is one moral duty against another – the duty to preserve life against the duty to prevent avoidable harm. Because this is a balancing of different duties, there is no precise moral calculus which can do the job for us. How bad does an evil have to be, before we would take an innocent life to prevent it? I have no precise formula to offer; but I do suggest that there could be an evil bad enough to justify the killing of the innocent.

Let me give just one example. A crowd of people is sitting in a park, unaware that a maniac is driving towards them in a large truck, intending to kill them all. You have with you a bazooka – a shell-firing gun, which can destroy the truck and everyone in it – and no other means of stopping it. But in the truck are the maniac's wife and children, innocent victims of his madness. Would you blow up the truck? If it is your family in the park, would that make a difference?

In the last world war, and in many wars, there are many similar examples of soldiers using civilians as hostages, or as shields between them and the enemy, or as passengers on munitions trains, to stop the Resistance attacking them. As Vitoria said long ago, of the case of siege, in such cases, where the slaughter of the innocent is a necessary part of attacking the enemy, and is not chosen for its own sake, it is permissible. Thus it is that in extreme emergency, when there is no other way to avert final disaster; where the enemy cannot be stopped without killing the innocent; and where such killing is not chosen except as an unavoidable part of the action of attacking the enemy; there the principle of discrimination, in one of its main forms ('not killing the innocent') may be overridden.

Principle of double effect

NUCLEAR IMPLICATIONS

The relevance of this to nuclear warfare is clear. It is accepted that there is no defence against nuclear attack by conventional forces. Indeed, there is no defence at all, in the sense that we could not physically prevent such a missile attack. The only options we have against an enemy who is prepared to use nuclear weapons are to surrender or to try to eliminate his launching-sites with nuclear weapons of our own. Any attempt

58

to launch a nuclear attack on him, however, will necessarily result in large numbers of innocent deaths, since nuclear weapons are inherently indiscriminate in their effects. In such a case, killing the innocent is not just a foreseen consequence of our action; it is a necessary part of the action itself. Though we may devoutly wish we could avoid it, we cannot. It is in this situation, where we might face obliteration as a people, that I would think it permissible to launch a nuclear response, if that response had any hope of preventing our obliteration.

But this is only the beginning of the nuclear debate. For now it will be said that, even if indiscriminate killing can be justified in ultimate extremity, where the very survival of a people is at stake, this is a purely theoretical point, which misperceives the scale of the problem. For we are not just talking about some killing of private citizens who have the misfortune to live near missile silos. With the number of nuclear weapons in the world today, we are talking about the destruction of whole countries, of future generations by genetic mutation, of totally uninvolved countries by fall-out, of the structure of civilized life itself. A nuclear response would not defend our nation; it would destroy us, along with the rest of the world. It would be suicide. That is what is meant by those who say that nuclear weapons cannot in fact be used in defence at all.

This brings us to consider the principle of proportion. Detailed formulations of the principle are rarely satisfactory; but broadly speaking, it asserts that the evil caused by war must be less than the evil it avoids. Once again we have the difficulty of weighing diverse values – in this case, we usually have to weigh the values of justice against the values of utility. That is, we have to weigh the injustices of aggression, destruction of culture, deprivation of freedom and democracy, against the suffering and deaths caused by resistance. The evil of war must be proportionate to the aims of war. As the Cambridge philosopher Henry Sidgwick put it, what is ruled out is 'any mischief which does not tend materially to the end, nor . . . of which the conduciveness to the end is slight in comparison with the amount of mischief'. There is no hard and fast rule here. But most people would agree that, if it was not possible to defend oneself successfully, or if the prosecution of war actually made the sustaining of a just society impossible, then the principle of proportion would be clearly contravened.

Now an all-out nuclear war cannot be fought to win and to preserve justice and freedom. In such a war, there could be no winners, no survivors. All organized life would be destroyed. Nuclear warfare is not just mildly indiscriminate; it is so vastly indiscriminate that it puts the whole world at risk. It is therefore also disproportionate to any conceivable end (except the end of national suicide, perhaps). A nuclear response could not prevent defeat. It can prevent victory; but only at the cost of the whole world. All-out nuclear war must consequently stand unequivocally condemned, under the principles of the 'Just War' tradition. It is morally unjustifiable.

That may seem to be the end of that. Unfortunately, however, we have only succeeded in impaling ourselves upon yet another dilemma; one which, because of its importance and seriousness, might well be called the ultimate moral dilemma. The dilemma is that we have a duty to repel or prevent armed aggression, which threatens the fundamental rights of people for whom we have a special responsibility. But we also have a duty not to engage in an all-out nuclear war. It is devoutly to be hoped that both those duties may peacefully co-exist, now and forever. But suppose that we have an enemy with nuclear weapons. If we have none, he can quickly impose his will upon us by using them until we surrender, as we will have to, sooner or later. That, after all, is how the United States terminated the war with Japan so quickly. If we are to fulfil our duty of defence, we need to be able to reply in kind. I take this point to be quite decisive – without nuclear weapons, there is no defence against an aggressive enemy who has them. That is why the first atomic bomb was manufactured – because it was feared that Hitler might get one, and become invincible. That is why the Russians developed nuclear weapons – afraid of an American attack on the Communist system in Russia.

The possibility remains in our world, and will remain for the foreseeable future, that some aggressive dictator could develop a nuclear weapon, and use it to impose his will on other states. It looks as though any state which fears an aggressor with nuclear arms, will feel it permissible to develop them, too. So we get what is called 'horizontal proliferation' – more countries developing a nuclear capability – as well as 'vertical proliferation' – the constant attempt by nuclear-armed states to achieve a weapons superiority, by continued technological innovation and arms build-up. As a result of this process, we already have

60

enough nuclear weapons in existence to destroy the world a number of times. But it follows that any use of such weapons by one of the super-powers – or, indeed, any form of war between them at all – could lead to an escalation to all-out nuclear war. Thus there is a finite probability that any form of defence, by one major nuclear power against another, could lead to all-out nuclear war. Now the dilemma becomes acute; we have a duty to defend, and a duty not to engage in all-out nuclear war; yet nuclear defence seems to put us on a course towards such war.

The obvious way to avoid this dilemma is to stop the process at some point short of all-out war. What we have to do is to threaten to cause a degree of damage to the enemy which will be unacceptable to him, against which he will have no defence, and which will be seen by him as a credible threat (one we may well carry out). If we have enough nuclear weapons to destroy his major military installations and their adjacent territories, that does seem to be the minimum threat necessary to deter a nuclear first strike; and it is credible, in the sense that it could provide for the survival of our remaining peoples. The prospect is indeed a horrifying one; but there is no other way of defence against a nuclear attack or threat of attack. And we must bear in mind that, if what we threaten is indeed credible, unstoppable and unacceptably damaging, no rational enemy could attack us. Deterrence of this sort is vastly preferable to actual fighting. It is easy to see the attraction of having such a formidable deterrent that we will never actually need to fight an enemy attack. There is much truth in the adage that we will only be attacked if we are seen to be weak enough to make a fairly easy prey. If we are so strong that nothing could stop us from inflicting an unacceptable degree of damage on any enemy, we will be immune from attack, except from a suicidal madman.

This notion of a balanced, limited nuclear deterrent seems to be one which falls within the limits of the "'Just War' theory, even if it is at the horrifying extremity of justifiability. I therefore think that it is unduly naive and simplistic to say that the possession or use of nuclear weapons could never be justified, in any conceivable circumstance. It seems to me likely that the possession of nuclear weapons is such a strong deterrent that it makes any direct conflict between the super-powers and their client-states extremely improbable – and we must remember the appalling suffering and destruction any conventional war would cause, in the modern world. It thus decreases the likelihood of any war between those powers. However, if even a conventional war should occur, there is no point in pretending that countries with a capacity to make nuclear weapons might not then begin to do so. There is simply no way of banning nuclear weapons from the face of the earth. In that sense, there is no alternative to nuclear deterrence anyway. The monster has been unleashed; and we must discover ways to live with it.

Nevertheless, the present world-situation does give genuine cause for concern. All the nuclear powers are signatories to the Non-Proliferation Treaty of 1968; they are thereby committed to negotiate in good faith for the cessation of the nuclear arms race at an early date and for nuclear disarmament under strict and effective international control. The commitment to nuclear disarmament exists for at least three main reasons: there are far more weapons in existence than are licensed by the notion of limited deterrence; the horror of nuclear war is so great that anything to decrease its probability must be tried; and the horizontal proliferation of such weapons increases the risk that they may actually be used again.

MORALLY UNJUSTIFIABLE

I have spoken of a limited deterrent. There will be much argument about exactly how large this will be; but it will certainly not be large enough to obliterate the earth. There is nothing very limited about that. And yet both super-powers have enough weapons to do just that. Moreover, the Americans at least used to have, and the Russians still have, a policy of releasing all their weapons at the earliest moment of a nuclear war. That is exactly the all-out war which is morally unjustifiable. And even as a form of deterrence, it is scarcely credible; for anyone would have to be mad to destroy the world. This is often called the paradox of deterrence – you threaten to do something quite immoral, if your enemy does x; in the belief that your threat is the only thing which will prevent him doing x; and that, accordingly, you will never have to implement it.

This is not a case of threatening to do the lesser of two evils; there would not be such a great moral problem about that. You are threatening to do the greater evil – since the destruction of the world is worse than the destruction of your country. Now, if you could know for certain that your threat would stop x occurring, the threat (which is, in itself, nowhere near as evil as actually doing what you threaten) would be morally justifiable. That is, making the threat, though an evil, would be the lesser of two evils.

Proponents of Mutually Assured Destruction argue that it is as good as certain that the threat of total destruction will prevent a nuclear first strike; nothing else could be sure to prevent it; and so a very great evil is averted by the threat to do something even worse; and that is morally justifiable. That is so. But the fact remains that it is not, of course, absolutely certain that a first strike will be deterred. The reason for this is the obvious insanity of actually destroying the world. An enemy might reasonably think that the threat of retaliation is a bluff – especially if we make it known that we regard the implementation of the threat as totally unjustifiable. The very scale of the deterrent might lead him to attack, gambling that we could never bring ourselves to use it. It would be a gamble – this is what the theory of deterrence relies on for its effect. But it is nevertheless no longer certain that our threat will deter attack.

Now the argument is more difficult. Your threat to do something terribly evil only makes it *likely* that it will prevent the action which will lead you to realise your threat. The less certain your threat is to deter, the less justifiable the threat becomes. The terrifying equation of deterrence is that you have to balance a low probability of immense harm against a higher probability of a very great, but still certainly less harm. Not surprisingly, estimates will differ about when the deterrent threat becomes too dangerous. But it is apparent that such an equation is logically unstable – that is, the variables it works with are so ill-defined and subject to personal judgement that miscalculation is all too easy. In a time of *détente*, there is little to worry about. But in a time of international tension and belligerence, it would take only one miscalculation to end the world. That is not a risk we should live with, for longer than we have to. There is an urgent moral imperative to move out of that situation.

It is largely in the attempt to do so that NATO doctrines of 'flexible response' were developed. According to this doctrine, we would not move straight away to all-out nuclear war. There would be a number of stages of nuclear use, from battlefield nuclear shells on European territory, in order to destroy an invading army, to limited strikes on enemy territory; and only when all else fails, to the final assured destruction of the enemy. The aim was to make the deterrent threat more credible; but it has not been perceived in that way – and deterrence is more about what people perceive than about what you intend. To begin with, Russia does not accept such a doctrine; her policy is still to retaliate with all force against any use of nuclear weapons, however small. Secondly, they perceive this doctrine as a willingness to engage in a limited nuclear war in Europe. Together with the technological advances which shorten reaction-times and increase accuracy, this seems to make nuclear conflict, perhaps by the foolishness of some field commander or even by accident, more likely.

I believe much of the Russian response to such moves to be propaganda to weaken the North Atlantic Alliance. Nevertheless, the fact is that the possibility of all-out war remains. And the likelihood of it occurring does increase if one side in the conflict does not believe in flexible response, and if the other side seems to be prepared to use nuclear weapons to prevent even an overwhelming conventional attack (and that is the NATO doctrine of 'first use'). For that reason, the doctrines of first use and flexible response fail to solve the problem of the instability of the nuclear equation. For they make an actual use of nuclear weapons more likely; and, given the Russian attitude (even allowing for propaganda), that does make escalation to all-out nuclear war possible. We cannot be content with any doctrine which makes the unjustifiable more likely, by however little.

MONSTER

It is therefore imperative to dismantle the apparatus which makes all-out war possible, and to cease relying on the threat to resort to it. If we must live with the monster of nuclear weaponry, we must at least cage it securely. But how is this to be done? In a situation where each super-power can destroy the other, it seems that the minimum that sanity requires is a Comprehensive Test Ban Treaty; an end to further development of nuclear weapons which could be seen as offensive; an end to the impossible search for 'parity' of nuclear weapons; an end to reliance on the first use of nuclear weapons to counter conventional attack; and the beginning of deep cuts in the stockpiles of the super-powers.

I have outlined the arguments of the 'Just War' theory, and tried to show how the theory could permit a limited and defensive nuclear deterrent. But what it does not permit is the holding of an unlimited nuclear deterrent, where there is any likelihood of it being used. And it does not permit any longer a search for nuclear superiority which can only fuel an unending arms-race.

The major problem arises when all apparently agree that it is imperative to disarm, mutually and verifiably; and no-one seems to do so. I suggest that the deterrence equation, while defensible in theory, is weakened by two considerations – one, that the very incredibility of total destruction makes it less certain that the deterrent threat will work; and two, that there is something else which will prevent a nuclear first strike just as certainly and more credibly. That is, of course, limited deterrence; sufficient to cause unacceptably high, not total destruction. In the immediate future, then, we should aim to maintain a limited nuclear deterrent. We can give up the search for parity, and the fear that we may be falling behind in the arms race. That is irrelevant, since a race to create more and more incredible deterrents is not worth entering.

We can encourage both Russia and America to make unilateral cuts, if necessary, since it will have no effect on their deterrent capacity. In other words, we can concentrate on strengthening our conventional defence, and hold our nuclear forces well back, at a limited level, and solely for the purpose of discouraging a nuclear attack upon us by threatening an unacceptably damaging response.

I do not suggest that this is enough. It is an urgent requirement not to be content with the minimum that is permissible, but to work much more positively to reduce any threat of nuclear use, by a much more complete nuclear disarmament. But that must be a mutual process. It is in this sense that I am a 'multilateralist'. But there are steps that can be taken now, both to start the multilateral process going by a clear renunciation of the goal of nuclear parity at every level; and to stabilize the deterrence equation by decreasing the scale of destruction a retaliatory nuclear strike would cause. I believe that when the arguments are set out clearly, a moral obligation emerges to act at once, and without conditions, to make all-out (unlimited) nuclear war impossible.

I do not think it makes sense to declare, as the World Council of Churches did recently (27 July 1982) that 'the production and deployment as well as the use of nuclear weapons are a crime against humanity'; and at the same time to hold that nuclear deterrence is acceptable as a temporary measure. Nor do I think it makes sense to hold that all-out nuclear war could destroy the world, and yet to co-operate in acts which increase its likelihood. There is a form of nuclear deterrence which is unacceptable – mutually assured destruction. Since it is also incredible, we should move away from it unconditionally – by such things as deep cuts, working towards a policy of 'no first use' in Europe, the implementation of a freeze on the production of new weapons, and so on. And there is a form of nuclear deterrence which is acceptable, while being highly undesirable – limited, balanced deterrence. It is an obligation to move away from that too, but in this case, the obligation is conditional upon mutual agreement.

In this paper, I have not hesitated to express my own views. But my main purpose has been to exhibit the structure of the arguments used in assessing the moral justifiability of nuclear deterrence. If only one thing is clear, it is that the issues are not simple and straightforward. Opinions are almost bound to modify, as we re-assess and try to balance the strength of the various arguments. One thing I have tried to stress is that there are risks, and there is moral unease, whichever way we choose. In this indecision and unease we see something important about the nature of morality. And perhaps we see why Christian faith cannot be identified with, or even founded upon, the moralism of the self-assured and the self-righteous.

5
POWER, COERCION AND MORALITY
Richard Harries

5. Power, coercion and morality

Deterrence works on the minds of potential adversaries. Its purpose is to convince them that the cost of any aggressive action would be unacceptably high. Within the NATO alliance this purpose is achieved by retaining the option to use nuclear weapons. Missiles in position, with men trained to use them, force a possible enemy to stop before taking a step that might be construed as hostile; and to conclude, on any rational assessment, that the destruction that could be unleashed would be out of proportion to any conceivable gain. The ethical aspect of a policy of nuclear deterrence has many dimensions, some ancient and a well considered part of the Just War tradition, others new. One perennial problem that has received far too little attention in recent discussion is the fact that all human relationships have a power factor. The neglect of this in *The Church and the Bomb* was particularly serious and resulted in a distorted view of the dilemma.

The power element is an inescapable feature of all human relationships at both an individual and, more particularly, at a group level. The struggle to dominate or avoid domination goes on ceaselessly and takes many forms from the simple power of one personality over another, to underlying economic realities. The writer Philip Toynbee decided to allow a commune to use his house. Eventually the commune got into a state of disarray and Philip Toynbee decided to repossess his home, despite the opposition of its inhabitants. In the journal he was keeping at the time Toynbee wrote this:

'I delivered a violent harangue, to which nobody spoke a single word in answer. It was Them and Us with a vengeance now; the sweet freaks and children of nature up against the angry proprietor whose only thought was to drive them all away and sell the empty house for a fat sum. A melancholy change. Or, as some would say, no change at all, but simply the true situation no longer disguised by kindly pretences from both sides.'[1]

Not all kindly, liberal-minded people are as aware as this. Living in a benign haze they often fail to see the harsh structures around which much social life is constructed. Or if they are aware of it at a theoretical level they, mercifully, do not often have the chance to experience the reality. In Nadine Gordimer's novel *July's People*,[2] Johannesburg has been taken over by forces of black liberation. A liberal white family have been rescued by their houseboy, July, and taken by him to his home village. The novel explores the feelings of the white couple who now suddenly find themselves dependent on a person who has been totally dependent on them for the previous fifteen years. The predicament they find themselves in is focused in a series of small details, for example, who keeps the keys of the landrover in which they have escaped? Or, for that matter, who now owns it, the white couple or their houseboy to whom they owe their lives and on whom they are now totally reliant for food and safety? The novel brings out well, in an undogmatic way, how the most altruistic people still share in the fruits of domination of the class or group to which they belong. Those who preached a social gospel in the 1920s and those who urged pacifism in the 1930s had to be taught the realities of power by Reinhold Niebuhr.[3] It appears that today the Church has almost totally failed to assimilate his message.

The word 'power' is vague and this reflects the fact that there are so many different forms of power. No definition can completely escape assumptions but the word will be defined here in as neutral a way as possible. *Power is the capacity to achieve a desired goal.* This leaves the question of the means whereby the desired goal is achieved open. Max Weber's definition also leaves the question of means open, though it stresses that the goal will be achieved even if there is opposition. '"Power" is the probability that one actor within a social relationship will be in a position to carry out his own will despite resistance, regardless of the basis on which this probability rests.'[4]

The possession of power, being in a position to carry out our will, having the capacity to achieve a desired goal, is not evil in itself. As human beings we all possess power to some degree, or we would not be here. Even a baby has the power to take in food and as it grows it develops power to walk and generally to obtain what it wants (always restricted of course by the power of others to get what they want). Our existence, our being, is inseparable from power of some kind and in some degree. The same is true of God.

DIVINE POWER

In recent decades there has been a tendency to underplay the notion of God's power. Within process theology there has been a healthy emphasis on God's persuasive love as opposed to his force. In W. H. Vanstone's *Love's Endeavour, Love's Expense*[5] there was a powerful attempt to see God's creation, as well as the Incarnation, as a Kenosis, or self-emptying. God, it was argued, does not have reserves of power over and above what he expends in creation; in that creation he totally drains or empties himself. The book is a moving attempt to make the moral element paramount in our understanding of God. This is absolutely right. Power by itself availeth nothing. As Simone Weil once put it, Christ could die and rise again three times in front of her and it would do nothing to win her allegiance as a moral being. Our response to God is, first and last, a moral response; that is, we see in him the source and standard of all that is good, true and beautiful.

Nevertheless, a powerless God is a logical nonsense. If God exists at all he has the power that is appropriate to his being as God. It belongs to God, and to God alone, to create *ex nihilo*. It belongs to God to transmute matter into the very stuff of eternity at the end of time. It belongs to God to raise Christ Jesus from the dead. The resurrection cannot be considered apart from the moral worth of the life and death of Jesus. It does not seek to impress by a display of naked power. But nor on the other hand is the resurrection simply the register of a change of outlook on behalf of the disciples. It is God doing what it is proper for God to do, bringing life from death. This is a power that belongs to his being, as it belongs to our being to understand and manipulate the forces of nature in order to build a civilization. Furthermore, it could be argued that without this power and a willingness to use it, God would not have been morally justified in creating the universe in the first place. It must be part of our moral evaluation of God that in bringing into existence sentient beings he had the power to bring about an ultimate state of affairs in which they would bless their creator for their existence.

71

Power is the capacity to achieve a desired goal. God has the capacity, it belongs to him as God, first to create the world and then to redeem it. But what means does God use? Persuasion or coercion? There is nothing wrong with force in itself. The morality of its use is determined by the object. Where the object is material, force is the appropriate means to employ. We use force to wield a cricket bat or a paint brush, a spade or a saw. So God creates the universe by the direct and unhindered operation of his will and in the case of material objects his will for them directly coincides with the operation of their being.

Where creatures have a mind and will, however, it is persuasion rather than coercion that is morally proper. This is true without qualification in God's dealings with his creatures in relation to himself. A forced love would be a contradiction in terms. It would not be love, for love by definition is a freely chosen delight in a person for their own sake. We deem it totally inappropriate and morally reprehensible for a parent to try to compel a child to love them. They might be able to force some response from an unwilling child but what they forced would not be love. The same is equally true in our relationship with God. Nevertheless the use of force for other purposes cannot be ruled out altogether on moral grounds. We deem it appropriate for example, and morally proper, if a parent insists that his child wear a luminous strap when cycling and that he back up this insistence with the threat of penalties. Out of love for the child and a concern for his safety the parent may have to use sanctions. For it may be only in this way that the life of the child is preserved. Or again, in a family with a number of children, it may only be possible to maintain the order that is necessary for communal living through the use of penalties. It may be essential, for example, that the family sit down to a meal together. The mother has a job and the ordered structure of the household demands it, even apart from questions of family fellowship. So the children have to drop their tasks, even worthy ones like homework, in order to come to a meal. It may on occasion prove necessary to use sanctions to achieve this.

Penalties, or the threat of penalties, are not incompatible with love. They may be necessary both for our safety and in order to harmonize the often conflicting desires and wills of persons in community. But what is the true nature of these penalties? Sometimes the impression is given both in the case of human beings and of God that they are the arbitrary infliction of pain by someone who has been offended or outraged. This picture is a travesty. The moral justification of penalties arises from the fact that all actions have consequences. A person in a pique, for example, takes it out on another member of the family. This other person drives off in a car and because they are upset they have an accident. This accident has all kinds of consequences and so it goes on in an endless series of causal connections. The fact that all our actions have consequences is sometimes unpleasant but it provides the basis of all our planning, thinking and attempts to act responsibly. Because, within limits, we can predict what the consequences of our actions will be, we can plan for the future and make rational decisions about it. God's justice, seen apart from his love, consists simply in letting events take their course; in letting human beings suffer the natural consequences of their deeds. Sometimes, perhaps more often than not, it is other people rather than we ourselves who suffer the ill consequences of our ill deeds.

This fact brings to the fore two other features of our existence which need to be taken into account. The first is that we are so made by God that loving behaviour is designed to lead to our fulfilment and flourishing. He has created us not so much that virtue will be its own reward, though in a sense it is, but that virtue will lead to the well-being and eternal blessedness of our nature.[6] The second feature is the solidarity of mankind both in sin and in Christ. Although at the moment we only grasp this through the use of a loving imagination it is ontologically true that if one suffers all suffer.

Taking into account these considerations therefore, the essence of punishment is letting people suffer the consequenes of their actions. But the loving mind does not want this to happen to the beloved. A loving parent does not want a child to suffer the consequences of his carelessness by being run over. Nor does a loving mother want her family to suffer the consequences of total anarchy. This means that if a child fails to wear a luminous strap for safety, or if children fail to turn up to the planned family meal, there are penalties. These may be minor or severe, though usually they take the form of loss of pocket money or being made to do extra washing up or being forbidden the use of the bicycle for a period. But in essence their nature is the same. They are an anticipation, a foretaste, of the unpleasantness of the predicted consequences of the action in order to bring it home and to prevent it coming about. Punishment, whether it is in the home, or in prison or in purgatory, may serve a number of functions including deterring other people or safeguarding others. But these functions are only justified on the basis of the central fact about punishment. It is, *for love's sake*, an anticipation of the harmful consequences of a harmful action, in order to avert the full consequences.

COERCION AND LOVE

It can now be seen that properly understood coercion has a place in divine love. For coercion is simply letting people see something of the consequences of their actions. When a parent says to a child 'If you don't wear your luminous safety strap, you won't be allowed to ride your bike in the dark' this could be called a threat. It could be objected to on the grounds that the child is being forced by the threat of something unpleasant to do something against his will. Nevertheless what that parent says is a perfectly proper expression of love; and this form of expression has a place in God.

Martin Luther pictured God ruling the world in two ways. With one hand he offered people the love of Christ and by winning a free response to this love brought people into the church. With the other hand he maintained the fabric of society through coercion. So, according to Luther, society was held together in two ways; by Christians who did what had to be done out of love; and by coercion, so that society kept going with some degree of order whether people willed it or not. Modern Lutheran theology has tended towards modifications of Luther's 'Two Kingdoms' but it highlights an essential distinction. On the one hand, as was discussed earlier, love to be love must be freely chosen. A person, of their own volition, comes to delight in someone else, whether that person is another human being or God. This love cannot be forced or it loses its essential character. It can only be won and the only way it can be won is through the persuasive power of love itself. On the other hand whether people are loving or not society has somehow to be held together. If life is to go on at all the fabric of society has to be maintained, human communities have to be ordered.

What the preceding paragraphs have tried to show is that the coercive power which is necessary for this ordering is not a denial of love but the appropriate expression of love under certain conditions. This coercive power is wielded by human beings but if ultimately it is God who rules the universe, if God is responsible for this side of life as well as for the more intimate tender side, then it is necessary to show that such coercion is compatible with love. Martin Luther said that if he was attacked when he was going about his business as a minister of the Gospel he would follow the injunction of the Sermon on the Mount and not resist. This seems perfectly proper. The Gospel can be neither propagated nor defended by force. There is something utterly out of character about missionaries defending themselves with guns. On the other hand Luther said that if he was attacked as a citizen he might very well defend himself for then he would be doing his part in maintaining the order of society. In practice the distinction might be hard to make but at the theoretical level it is both clear and legitimate.

It is for this reason and on the basis of this distinction that Christians should reject the 'crusade' mentality. People sometimes talk about defending Christian civilization or Christian values against atheistic communism. But though civilization of all kinds can and should be defended against forces which seek to destroy them, what is distinctively Christian cannot and should not be so defended. This sounds a hard doctrine. What is most precious to us we most want to defend. Nevertheless what is Christian can only be championed on the basis of persuasive love. What has to be defended are the conditions which make human life of any kind possible.[7] The good has to be freely chosen but the conditions which make it possible for the good to be chosen have to be maintained. These conditions cannot be upheld simply on the basis of goodwill; coercion is necessary both within states and between them.

Further exploration is necessary as to why coercion is needed not simply on an occasional basis but as an essential, continuing constituent of human society. In classical Christian realism its necessity is attributed to the fall. Man is a fallen creature, a sinner, who is always likely to wreck every new constellation of good. Nevertheless the necessity of coercion for the organization of human community does not arise simply out of this aspect of human nature. Three other features are enough to account for it. First, human beings pursue their own interests. Secondly, they have only a limited capacity to take into account the interests of others. Thirdly, when human beings are organized into groups, both these tendencies are accentuated and made into a cardinal principle. All these features belong to human life as such and are not in themselves the result of any fall.

Thus, it is necessary for the survival of both the individual and the species that creatures pursue their own interests; indeed it is a mark of vitality, of the will to struggle and survive, that they do so. If a baby did not have enough self-interest to reach for the bottle, it would die. If the schoolboy, or girl, does not have enough self-interest to stand up for himself or herself, he or she is likely to become psychologically squashed. That we have only a limited capacity to take into account the interests of others is not the sign of some dramatic fall from grace but an indication of our immaturity. We have been made, by God, part of the animal kingdom, with enough self-interest to survive, yet with a dawning capacity to be aware of the needs and claims of others. It is the heart of the challenge of life that this capacity grows. But the picture is an Irenaean rather than an Augustinian one. We are infants struggling through to maturity rather than perfect beings thrown out of paradise. Then, when it comes to group life, the willingness to strive for the interest of the group becomes a virtue; the unwillingness to take into account the needs of other groups not necessarily a vice. For example a university that seeks to engage the most able research students is not acting in a reprehensible manner. The fact that it does not let them go to a minor college struggling for survival is not necessarily a vice.

A number of modern novelists, as well as most of human history including most modern history, indicate all too clearly the truth that man is 'fallen'. Nevertheless, although this makes the necessity of coercion in human affairs more insistent, this necessity can be accounted for in other terms as well. It may be useful to do this, if only for the reason that some modern people find it impossible to make sense of assertions such as 'man is fallen' or else they are alienated by such language. Coercion is necessary because human beings pursue their own interests, they have only a limited capacity to transcend those interests for a greater good, and in organized group life these tendencies become normative.

76

It is, for example, all too easy to understand how, if one was born on a kibbutz one would be fighting passionately for Israel, and if one was born in a Palestinian refugee camp one would be fighting with equal conviction for the PLO. Both sides are imbued with a will to survive; for both sides the individual will to survive is invested with the status of a virtue when it is put at the service of the cause; on neither side is sympathy towards the other side's point of view prized or encouraged. Both sides no doubt share the general lot of fallen mankind. Yet less mysterious than that is the simple fact that both sides have very different perceptions, in particular very different perceptions about where right lies. In this situation goodwill is desperately necessary but a solution is not going to be achieved by goodwill alone. When a political solution is found, it will be one that will have to be enforced; enforced perhaps by outside powers on the parties to the dispute and by the leaders of each side on their own extremists.

According to Marxist analysis economic forces are the determinants of human history. Each class inevitably pursues its own economic interests. Yet it can be questioned whether the economic factor is always the pre-eminent one. In early feudal society it was a combination of military and priestly power that was usually successful. The economic power of these castes was a consequence not a cause of their dominance.

According to some people, (eg. Nietzsche), human beings are characterized by a basic will-to-power so that through every means at our disposal we are engaged in a ceaseless struggle to dominate or avoid being dominated. There is clearly much truth in this analysis, as there is in the Marxist one, but again it does not cover all the constituents of a conflict situation. There is for example the element of insecurity. Israel desires, apparently, to retain the West Bank. She has been extremely reluctant to give up territory captured in recent wars. Outsiders often see this in terms of her expansionist ambitions. She herself sees it in terms of a need to be secure. The fact is that the defensive/aggressive mentality, the desire to be secure and the need to expand a little in order to re-main secure, are so closely intertwined it is often impossible to separate them.

GROUP SELF-INTEREST

The fact remains that however we account for it, whether in terms of economic determinism, a will-to-power, or a legitimate desire for security, human groupings tend to pursue their own interests whilst only partially taking into account the perceptions and interests of other groupings. The failure to realize this was one of the most notable weaknesses in *The Church and the Bomb*. The authors of the report argued that Soviet defence policy was not aggressive and that it only looked as though it was because of their intention to strike hard and quickly if a war did break out. Yet this fact, even if true, should not lead to less vigilance in relation to them any more than a comparable conclusion in relation to the USA should lead to less vigilance in relation to them. For all major powers have an incipient imperialist tendency.[8] The defensive/aggressive mentality in which we all share leads them to strive for the maximum rather than the minimum security. So the Soviet Union seeks to retain control over her satellite states, Poland, East Germany, Hungary and so on. She seeks to gain control in other states on her borders, as in Afghanistan and she generally seeks to win friends and influence people throughout the world. None of this is in the least surprising, particularly, as the report rightly shows, the Soviet Union has the longest border in the world to secure and she has been both invaded and harassed by other powers during the last sixty years.

What is true of the Soviet Union is true in one way or another of America. One of the major ways in which the two super powers seek power and influence in the modern world is through arms transfers. America and the Soviet Union, who between them have over 80 per cent of the market, pursue their rivalry in the developing world by exporting enormous quantities of arms. Arms transfers have doubled in the last decade and three-quarters of the trade goes to the developing world. In a number of regions, such as the Middle East, American and Soviet arms transfers are a mirror image of one another. In the modern world invasion of another territory is highly dangerous (it might precipitate a nuclear war) and it is more difficult to retain bases in foreign countries. So superpower rivalry takes a different form. Each seeks client states, countries dependent upon it, who can be relied on to maintain and pursue its interests.[9]

Major powers pursue their own political interests. They seek to secure their borders and this includes having states on the borders. They tend to move in if there is a power vacuum. Similarly if there is instability in a particular region each major power will have a particular concern about it, the Soviet Union to aid 'forces of liberation', America to strengthen forces of stability. Given this ceaseless struggle for power and influence, this endless hard-nosed jostling for position, how can the twin goals of justice and peace be best achieved in the world?

Firstly, it must be acknowledged that there are legitimate security needs of all states, even traditional enemies and potential adversaries. From the foregoing analysis it is clear that the world in which we live is one in which all states have, and will continue to have for the foreseeable future, security needs. How these needs are met will vary. At the moment they take the form of a defence capability or membership of an alliance which has promised support in the event of being attacked. In some parts of the world there are signs of an approach to security on a regional basis. One day, pray God, it will be possible to achieve security on a world-wide basis in a way which avoids the endless warring of sovereign and suspicious states on the one hand, and the potential tyranny of a world government on the other. But until that time comes all states have to take steps, either on their own or in company with others, to safeguard their security. This must be affirmed, without qualification, even about one's most dire adversary.

Secondly, attempts must be made to achieve a rough parity of power between adversaries.[10] Power was earlier defined as the capacity to achieve a desired goal. The goal in this case is security from external attack. The means by which this is obtained is through convincing potential aggressors that the cost of any aggression would be out of proportion to any conceivable good that could be obtained by it. There are a number of forms of power that can be utilized in the world to ensure peace and justice, such as economic coercion and persuasion, particularly when linked to traditional diplomatic skills. These skills tend to be underrated in relation to military strength but they are vital for international stability. The world contains innumerable political problems, often overlapping with one another. Above all these need political and diplomatic skills through which alone the many conflicting requirements of the international order can be brought together into an acceptable compromise. Nevertheless force and diplomacy go hand in hand. Coercion, including military coercion, remains an essential constituent of world order.

The purpose of a military capability is to convince a potential aggressor that aggression would unleash unacceptable damage. It forces other states to stop and count the cost before undertaking any action that might be construed as hostile. There are many types of coercion, most of them morally repugnant. It was earlier suggested, however, that not all coercion has this character.[11] All actions have consequences and it is not necessarily morally wrong to bring home to people what the consequences of their actions might be. For the Christian believer this truth is grounded in an ultimate state of affairs where the full consequences of our actions as human beings are known and suffered. When a state makes it clear through its possession of a defence capability that it will resist attack it is simply spelling out the fact that actions have consequences and that it is part of the moral character of the universe that they should.

There is often talk of a nuclear or military 'threat'. The use of the word 'threat' in this context is misleading. A threat is something we abhor on moral grounds. But a military capability, including a nuclear one, is only a threat to states contemplating aggression. Otherwise it is simply in existence as a reminder that events have consequences. The law of the land, with its penalties, is not a threat to those who keep the law. But it stands as a reminder that, for example, drunken driving can lead to deaths and those caught drunk in charge will suffer, through imprisonment, something of the suffering they inflicted or might have inflicted on other people.

The analogy with the law of the land is of course in some ways a simplistic one. On the whole within a country people know what the law is. Within the international order there are endless disputes with very different perceptions about what is the right and the wrong. Within a country the law makes an attempt to be impartial and it is administered by an authority that stands above the parties in a dispute. In the international order the parties take the law into their own hands for the only higher authority, the United Nations, has no power at the moment to enforce its authority. Nevertheless, what is at stake in the international order, as much as within a country, is the moral law; not simply international law, but moral law grounded finally in the being of God himself. However mistaken nations may have been in their understanding of the rights and wrongs of a particular issue, however often deceived in self-righteously abrogating to themselves the role of law-enforcers when they were in fact law breakers, the international order no less than the national order is based upon moral law. This means both that actions have consequences and that it is part of the moral character of the universe that they should. Any state with a military capability that is genuinely defensive is a standing reminder of this. Potential adversaries are aware that any act of aggression would lead to unacceptable damage being inflicted upon them . This is preeminently true of relationships between nuclear powers but it is also true of all military forces. For it is the primary purpose of all military force, not just nuclear force, to deter.

It was earlier argued that power, understood as the capacity to achieve a desired goal, was not in itself an evil. On the contrary it belongs both to divine and human nature that we are able to obtain something of what we want. If we did not have this capacity we would not exist. There is a positive aspect even to military power and the situation of a balance of power. This can be seen most easily at an individual level. When two people are roughly equal in wealth or status or mental ability there is more likely to be a basic respect for one another than when there is gross disparity. Human beings have a tendency to dominate or patronize one another. Where there is a rough equality – in the goods or qualities which both parties respect – this tendency will be less likely to assert itself; the parties will be more likely to take one another's needs and interests seriously. What is true at the individual level applies in relationships between groups. There is a proper pride and status that belongs to every nation. This cannot be purchased by military might and the attempt to do this is always disastrous, as was the case with Iran under the Shah. Nevertheless, a defensive capability is a necessary and proper component of nationhood. There is a popular inclination to think that non-aggressive nations like Switzerland or Sweden have no forces at all. This is not true: Sweden spends more per capita on defence than France, Great Britain or West Germany.

CHRISTIAN ELEMENT

Even amongst those who have followed the argument with some degree of sympathy there will remain some unease. The line of thought has been very secular, it seems; where is the distinctively Christian element? Jesus told his followers not to follow the example of pagan rulers who make others feel the weight of their authority. 'It shall not be so amongst you.' Rather, his followers are to be like him, servants of others. This service led him to death on the cross although, according to one Gospel account, he could have summoned legions of angels to his assistance. This moving and distinctive attitude of Jesus took theological form after his death. Paul affirms that the weakness of God is stronger than the power of men. He praises Christ as the eternal Son of God who emptied himself to come amongst us as a man. As the Dean of King's College, Cambridge, put it to me:

> 'Don't you think that renunciation of worldly power and force is a major and substantive Christian thing, integral to NT Christology whether in the Mt/Lk temptation stories or Paul *passim*? It seems to be so to me, and to be a treasure in the Church's keeping which is now urgently needed as something more than a theological ornament, renunciation being a thing so difficult and so necessary that people need all the help they can get. I don't think there can be love (including political love) without renunciation. I don't think there can be salvation without it and fear that without it there is destruction – or so my Bible seems to say.'

This is elegantly put, and coming from a distinguished scholar represents a considered and not just a popular view of what the NT contains. Clearly John Drury is right about the connection between love and renunciation of power at the individual level. In personal relationships if another person tries to 'pull rank' or makes threats based on superior force or wealth; if he tries to be 'one up' through the assertion of superior mental abilities or culture; if in any way he tries to make the other person feel small or inferior – then we regard this as a failure of love. Indeed we have been so influenced by this understanding of love that we would also regard it as a failure of manners or elementary courtesy.

The crucial question is how far this is either possible or appropriate in dealings between groups. If we say that it is not appropriate then we seem to allow for a double ethical standard, one for our dealings with others when we meet them on a personal level and one for our dealings with them when they are part of a group, whether that group is a rival business, a trade union or a hostile country. Nevertheless there are real difficulties, not only in discovering exactly what Jesus meant, but in applying what he said in the contemporary world. The main difficulty has to do with the fact that his teaching was given in the light of his expectation about the imminence of the Kingdom of God. Some scholars deny that this was part of the teaching of Jesus himself and they attribute it to the early Church. Others so understand the nearness of the kingdom that they imply Jesus would have taught the same truths in the same way, even if he had thought that the world would continue on the same course for several thousand years.

The position taken here is that Jesus did think that the kingdom, the decisive rule of God in human affairs, was near and that his ethical teaching has to be seen in integral relationship to that conviction. In other words if he had believed that human society would continue in its old way for thousands of years he would have balanced his teaching by more emphasis on what he took for granted, namely the law of the Old Testament.

The law of the Old Testament is applicable to the management of human society. Jesus assumes this. He does not so much overthrow it as call people to live in a way that transcends it, a way that will be vindicated very shortly, when God is clearly seen to reign on earth. When Jesus was asked to solve a dispute and said 'Who made me a divider and judge among you' he then called people to look at their basic motivation. This was his particular prophetic task. He did not imply that the law had no role. On the contrary the law clearly does have a role and it is precisely that of divider and judge in the case of disputes.

It cannot be denied that a Christian is called to live without dominating others and that if he finds himself in a position of dominance he has to find a way of meeting others on terms that are not a threat. Furthermore, it may very well be the witness of a particular Christian to assert the primacy of this approach in the political realm and not only in the sphere of personal relationships, for example, by being a conscientious objector. But this latter stand must be seen first and last as a witness to the ultimate rule of God in human affairs. It cannot, on Christian grounds, be regarded as a way of achieving desirable results in this world. Christ's death on the cross was not a way of bringing about the resurrection. The resurrection was a supernatural act of validation by God. The early Christian martyrs did not see their deaths as a way of hastening the kingdom. They cried 'How long O Lord?' but they did not think that there was a causal connection between their martyrdom and the coming of the end. Their deaths were primarily an act of witness. And this is how in the modern world renunciation of power or rights, in particular instances, should be viewed.

What has occurred in some quarters is a blend of pure Christian pacifism (the extreme form of renunciation of power) with Gandhi's concept of non-violent resistance. His technique was highly effective in India and also when used by Martin Luther King. It may also prove useful in other situations. Clearly also from a moral point of view it has much to recommend it. Nevertheless, for all its spiritual claims, it is still a technique (combining both coercive and non-coercive elements). Jesus believed that his heavenly father would bring in the kingdom, indeed was already bringing it in. He himself lived in that light and called others to do so. But it is God who brings in the kingdom. So it is that when Christians renounce power or rights this should be seen like martyrdom as an act of witness. There is no necessary causal connection between the renunciation and other events that follow. It could be that there is a favourable response. Sometimes at an individual level someone who comes across as 'all gift, no threat' disarms us; our barriers go down, our own tendency to dominate or impress is put aside and we try to relate to the other person as a person. But in relationship between groups such an outcome is much less likely. On the whole groups exploit weakness shown by others. This is not to deny that statesmen should seek to build up trust between nations by every means at their disposal. There are many ways in which this can and should be done and unilateral gestures of renunciation may have a place. But dramatic and wholesale unilateral renunciations of power would be both dangerous and immoral.

FOOLISH AND IMMORAL

One of the prime functions of government is to defend its people. Those who are elected to office in it are expected, rightly, to fulfil this function. A government that neglects this function is being not just foolish but immoral. The proper consideration in relation to any defence decision is whether it will genuinely help to preserve the security of the realm. It would be immoral, for example, for a Christian statesman to renounce a particular weapon if he genuinely believed that the weapon enhanced the defence of the realm or if he thought that holding onto the weapon would enable an agreement to be made with an adversary power which would bring real reductions in their weapons. That politician, as a Christian individual, might be tempted to make a moral gesture by renouncing the weapon. He might believe that by doing so he was witnessing to the truth of God's kingdom which is based on trust and not on force. Nevertheless, as a politician in government it would be immoral, a betrayal of trust, to renounce the weapon for those reasons. He must take only those steps which truly contribute to the security of the nation. His main concern therefore will always be with the practical consequences of suggested decisions. Will it or will it not have the desired effect? And this, despite all eschewing of moral gestures (unless they are calculated to serve a specific and predicted purpose) is a highly moral endeavour.[12]

In the fourth century the Christian Church ceased to be a small persecuted sect. Instead it became allied with government. The Roman army, once held at arm's length by Christians, became a Christian closed shop. Christians have always been divided in their attitude to this change in status under the emperor Constantine. Many Christians regard this as the great betrayal, the time when the rot set in. For others it is the point at which the Church grew up and took its share with others in maintaining the fabric of ordered society. Doing this means getting the hands dirty, taking responsibility in and for a coercive order. Augustine was not only a Bishop. He served as a magistrate meting out punishment.

There is no way national or international society can be maintained with some degree of justice, order and peace without coercion. It is possible for some Christians to renounce this totally. But this must be understood as a witness to an ultimate order that one day, under God, will be. It should not be seen as a means of bringing that order closer. *Some* renunciation in *some* situations may serve an important purpose. But such decisions must be made only on political grounds on the calculation that they will enhance the genuine security of the nation.

Multilateral weapons reduction, for example, is a bargaining process. Even given a genuine desire to achieve real reductions it is the nature of this process that each participant seeks to obtain the maximum concessions from the other side whilst conceding as little as possible itself. If one side thinks the other will concede something without anything being asked in return it is likely not to give anything in return. The difficulty is well illustrated in Kissinger's remark about trying to exact concessions from Israel: 'When I ask Rabin to make concessions, he says he can't because he is weak. So I give him more arms, and then he says he doesn't need to make concessions because Israel is strong.' A statesman, qua statesman, has to take this tendency into account. If the statesman is a Christian he has to take it into account no less than anyone else.

Luther made a distinction between the Christian ruled by God's persuasive love disclosed in Christ and the citizen ruled by God's coercive love working through the structures of society. Reinhold Niebuhr too made a distinction. In his case a distinction between what was possible between individuals motivated by love, where one person might give up what was rightfully due to him, and society made up of groups all pursuing their own interests. Niebuhr's analysis still retains much of its validity. Nevertheless, as he later acknowledged, and as Luther admitted, the true distinction is not between the individual and society or between the Christian and others. The source of the distinction is within oneself and within everyone, and it is between the capacity to transcend one's own interests in the interests of others and one's habitual reluctance to do so.

The simplest example of this problem is provided by taxation. Even if it were clearly explained to every citizen what taxes were being spent on, and an education programme was mounted to show how indispensable taxes are, how many people would pay the full amount they were assessed for if the collection was done on a voluntary basis with no penalties for those who defaulted? Not much tax would be collected in this way, even from avowed Christians. So tax, like everything else that is essential to the maintenance of society, is made the subject of laws. Laws, with the penalties for breaking them, exist to ensure that most people do most of the time what some people would do some of the time on a voluntary basis. Laws exist to close the gap between what in our better moment we choose to do and what for most of the time we are likely to do.

And what is true at a national level applies equally at the international. Coercion is necessary for the existence of an ordered human society and it is necessary for society as a whole at both a national and an international level because it is necessary for each one of us as individuals, whether or not we are Christian believers.

This essay has argued that although power has become a dirty word, it is an essential constituent of the being both of God and man. But if power is defined as the capacity to achieve a desired goal the crucial question concerns the method by which this goal is to be achieved. The only properly moral method of winning the free love of free creatures is the persuasive example of love itself. This is revealed in Christ and preached in the Gospel. Nevertheless, coercion, although it too has an ugly sound, implying immoral threats by immoral people, is not in itself always immoral. It belongs to the universe that actions have consequences and to the moral nature of the universe that ultimately we suffer the consequences of our own actions. 'God's coercive love' consists in allowing this to happen or making us aware that this will happen. It is primarily through this coercive love that God maintains the fabric of ordered society. In this way he establishes and upholds the conditions which make any kind of properly human life possible.

This coercive love is necessary for the just ordering of society because human beings pursue their own interests and have only a limited capacity to transcend them on behalf of the interests of others. Both these tendencies are deeply engrained in the working of human groups, not least in relationships between states. The fact that man is a 'fallen' creature is not the cause of this state of affairs but it accentuates its worst features. Within this kind of world the most likely way of reaching and retaining some degree of international stability is through a parity of power between potential adversaries. This power, the capacity to inflict unacceptable damage if attacked, forces nations to be careful and to avoid actions that could be construed as overtly hostile.

Balances of power are often precarious. Where the threat of destruction is almost total, as it is between the nuclear powers there is *some* hope that war can be averted. Where the threat of devastation is not total, as in the Middle East, a strong defensive capacity deters but peace is always fragile. Nevertheless in the world in which we live, the failure to deter is often a cause of war, as it was in the case of the Falklands, where the Argentinians were allowed to think that Britain had neither the capacity nor the will to resist. Balances of power as a way of keeping the peace have always been volatile. They must be accompanied by ceaseless political effort and sensitivity by all parties not simply to keep war at bay but to resolve the dispute which has given rise to the adversarial stance.

But power vacuums are even more dangerous. In a world where states are always seeking to extend their sphere of influence they are a standing temptation. Furthermore, a nuclear balance of power contains a feature that has never been present before. No side could win a nuclear war and it could never be in the interest of any power to fight a war against another power possessing nuclear weapons. This brings an element of stability into the balance that is totally new. Finally, utterly horrifying though nuclear weapons are, they act as a terrible warning to everyone involved, not just potential enemies, about the terrible consequences of going to war. Reflection on the reasons for which men have gone to war in the past, many of which now seem so trivial, can make us grateful for the horrifying reminder provided by the existence of nuclear weapons of the effects of human sin and folly. Never again will men be able to shrug off the thought of going to war; and in this there must be divine mercy as well as divine severity.[13]

Notes

1. Philip Toynbee, *Part of a Journey*, Collins, 1981, p. 230.
2. Nadine Gordimer, *July's People*, Jonathan Cape, 1981.
3. For an assessment of the continuing importance of Niebuhr see my re-review of *Moral Man and Immoral Society*, *MC*, New Series, Vol XXV, No 1, 1982.
4. Max Weber, *The Theory of Social and Economic Organization*, Oxford, 1947, p. 132.
5. W. H. Vanstone, *Love's Endeavour, Love's Expense*, Darton, Longman and Todd, 1980.
6. Since Law is 'grounded on the nature of things, and builds up acts that are for human happiness, it follows that its violation will incur contrary consequences, which will belong to the category of *malum poenae*, deprivation in a condition of being, or, in legal terms, penalty. With natural law these consequences are inevitable unless they can be arrested by the intervention of a third factor, divine mercy and the repair of the breach; there is an

interior connection between observance of the law and the good it will bring, between non-observance and the loss that will follow. Seek good and you will find it and all that goes with it, seek evil and you will find it and all that goes with it; the promise and the threat are implied in the very law, and are not arbitrarily attached to it by the ruling power.' Appendix 7, 'Coercion and Law' to volume 28 of the Blackfriars edition of the *Summa* of St Thomas Aquinas. Eyre and Spottiswoode, London.

7. 'Law is laid down for a number of people, of which the majority have no high standard of morality. Therefore it does not forbid all the vices, from which upright men can keep away, but only those grave ones which the average man can avoid, and chiefly those which do harm to others and have to be stopped if human society is to be maintained, such as murder and theft and so forth.' St Thomas Aquinas, *Summa* 1a2ae. 96,2. What is true of a nation is no less true in the international order.

8. 'The most conspicuous theme in international history is not the growth of internationalism. It is the series of efforts, by one power after another, to gain mastery of the states-system – efforts have been defeated only by a coalition of the majority of other powers at the cost of an exhausting general war.' Martin Wight, *Power Politics*, Leicester University Press, 1978, p. 30.

9. Andrew Pierre, *The Global Politics of Arms Sales*, Princeton, 1982.

10. Wight distinguishes several senses of the phrase 'Balance of Power', see chapter 5 of *Power Politics*. It can indicate an even distribution of power, a state of affairs in which no power is so preponderant that it can endanger the others. From this meaning comes the principle that power ought to be evenly distributed i.e. it passes from a descriptive to a normative use. The normative use, based on this description, is being advocated here.

11. *The Church and the Bomb* argued that both the use and the possession of nuclear weapons was immoral i.e. any coercion based on nuclear weapons would have to be ruled out on moral grounds. In my critique of the report in the Spring 1983 edition of *Christian* I argue that the possession, and use under some circumstances, of nuclear weapons does not violate the principles of discrimination and proportion in the absolute way suggested by *The Church and the Bomb*.

12. For this reason the recent motion by the General Synod of the Church of England condemning on moral grounds any first use of nuclear weapons and advocating on moral grounds a public declaration of no first use, can be criticized. If it is war itself, rather than simply nuclear war, which has to be avoided then a public declaration of no first use would be immoral for anyone who believed that this would make war more likely. See my article in the April-June 1983 edition of *Crucible*.

13. For an elaboration of the points see my 'Conventional Killing or Nuclear Stalemate?' in D. Martin & P. Mullen (eds), *Unholy Warfare*, Blackwell 1983.

6
A LAMB TO THE SLAUGHTER
Ulrich Simon

6. A lamb to the slaughter . . .

Pacifists differ in kind but have an identical aim, namely to achieve peace by peaceful means. Even in the nuclear age they envisage nuclear free zones and are prepared to work towards total disarmament unilaterally. Such a policy implies a submission to a power or powers which contemplate no similar action. Just as in a game of chess every move must lead towards a mate unless both sides agree on a draw so also in the game of war the very surrender of weapons and the possibility of retaliation amounts to capitulation. The unarmed will be taken over by the armed.

There is nothing very complicated in this equation. Military history gives countless examples of the mechanics of power. In the American Civil War, the North conquered the South by superior industrial power. The Boers in South Africa were defeated after reinforcements reached the British army. The First World War seemed to go on endlessly until the weight of American divisions offset the collapse of Russia. In the Second World War, Hitler's Germany fought to the bitter end and inevitable defeat after years of apparent triumph. Unconditional surrender coincided with total collapse in the field. Two atomic bombs forced Japan to yield. Ever since 1945 the study of conflict provides evidence for the supremacy of superior supplies.

Pacifists, however, intend to drop out of the race of mutual deterrence, and their reasons are plain and straightforward. They dismiss the examples from the past as irrelevant and with them the philosophy of deterrence. They are prepared to leave their own countries without defence since they will not devote money and effort to research in destructive weaponry. If faced by the threat of aggression, they either ignore its consequences or openly agree to submit to being conquered. They believe this policy to be warranted by the alternative, namely wholesale destruction of human beings, the civilized world, the earth with its living organisms. They universalize the slogan 'Better red than dead' to cover a global concern.

93

Paradoxically in this fight for unarmed surrender, some pacifists are seen to develop their own form of aggression. Although they pay lip service to non-violence they form movements which demonstrate violently. Revolutionary cells grow like cancer in pacifist organizations. The followers of Marx and Lenin could not wish for a better hunting ground than that of pacifist organizations. With their contempt for them and the notion of universal peace they push the unsuspecting unilateralists into their own camp. But even non-Marxists have a long tradition of violent non-violence. Christian sects fought for the kingdom of peace. Tolstoy is the inspired prophet of all social and religious movements which express their love for peace by violent means. 'Fight the good fight' intones an ambiguous concept for all lovers of peace. 'In the beginning was war', stated Heraclitus. Can the end be peace, with or without violence?

Naïvety does not provide an answer. The revolutionary knows what he is after: power and privilege. He anticipates the fruits of the great surrender in true Leninist fashion. The pacifist and nuclear unilateralist cannot state his aims beyond the surrender. The aims of peace, which the Leninist despises, are not specific but general, even utopian. But they fail to take into account the enemy. The unilateralist does not count the cost of capitulation. Naïvety leads to dishonesty when the immediate consequences of surrender are not envisaged. Western unilateralists curiously discount moral payment and loss. Empty shelves, unobtainable necessities, dire poverty, stripping of assets, control of labour, of movement, strict supervision, abrogation of civil rights, political codes of law and many more features can be sketched, not by the imagination but by direct observation of life in the Communist bloc. To submit to its mastery and thus to concede the end of freedom is not seeing 'reds under beds' but to look ahead realistically to the triumph of social patterns which equate freedom with bourgeois exploitation.

The Christian arrives at this position under double tension. On the one hand he professes a faith which appears to condone and even approve submission: on the other, he sees himself as a witness to a God revealed in Creation and Redemption and thus as a recipient of freedom. In this dilemma he is no longer concerned with the defence of material goods alone – though shelter, clothes, food, schools, amenities of all sorts protect man from total barbarism. The Christian may count the cost, even the highest cost, and still counsel submission. This is the heart of the debate now before us.

There are both continuities and discontinuities with the past. The great teachers of the Church never hesitated to support the righteous cause. In principle there could be a just war, and such a just war had to be won. True, not every war was just; hence the fairly demanding and rational definition of what made a war just. But there could be no doubt that far from advocating submission to the enemy the leaders lent their whole support to military enterprises against the enemy. Otherwise Islam, the Huns, the Turks would have won and swept away the last vestiges of Christendom. No Luther, no Zwingli, no Calvin would stand for a reform which emasculated the Christian cause in this world. The enemy had to be defeated or converted, but never submitted to.

Yet this tradition of strength has not lasted into the twentieth century. Even earlier on the religious wars in Europe left a residue of doubt. Who was the God to whom both sides could appeal for victory? How could guns be blessed by ministers of the same God? In any case, was the cost of war not exceeding the benefits victory could bring? In short, could there be a just war in the full sense of the definition?

Before the cataclysm of 1914-18 many voices could be heard in defiance, without actually advocating submission. Tolstoy's pacifism found its imitators. After the war 'to end all wars' a wave of anti-war feeling gripped the world. Schweitzer preached a gospel of the sacredness of all life and Gandhi practised resistance through non-violence. It seemed to many Christians that they had to learn from this secular gospel of reconciliation in which a common interest prevails and no one submits by force to any power.

This illusory world of co-operation and harmony failed from the start. Its adherents ignored the tensions in the world where nation, classes, races strove for mastery. The Western world entertained the pleasing fantasy that peace could always be negotiated. In the League of Nations no nation was expected to submit to another. In this optimistic climate Peace Pledge Unions annulled Christian pessimism. Hardly a writer dared sound an opposing note among the theologians before Word War II, for they had to atone for the terrible error of having lent their support to the battles of the First. When the economic crisis shook the foundations in the thirties, disarmament had in fact been under way and the way was paved for the aggressor. Hitler came to power in 1933.

Until war broke out in 1939, Christians still tended to opt for peaceful settlements in conflict. In endless discussions the pacifists defended their position by accepting the plaints and reasoning of the aggressor. The Versailles Treaty had been unjust; German claims were not without substance. Pacifists and politicians favoured a policy of appeasement as if the voracious appetite of the aggressor could be satisfied by concessions. They refused to detect the demonic criminality which led Hitler to prepare for war. Slowly the awareness of the threatening peril dawned, though the propaganda for peace increased. A mere rump of religious pacifists would have preferred capitulation to the Nazi tyranny when England remained alone in the fight in 1940, but apart from them, only the Communists and Fascists were eager to 'submit' to the new masters of Europe.

The Nazi terror of 1940–45 does not stand alone in the twentieth century. A vast catalogue of outrages has been added since in most parts of this sad planet. The whole pacifist ideology has been destroyed and has sharpened the issue of resistance and submission. Even during the climax of pacifist utopian thinking it was admitted by most that criminal violence must be contained. The policing of neighbourhoods was intended to check outbursts of criminality, and the courts were deemed sufficient to deal with the most serious offences. But this reasonable stance never envisaged that the police and the courts would be in the hands of hooligans, mobsters, and sadists, who were being used in an hierarchical system of administering murder. The Nazi pattern, largely copied from the GPU, operated under the competent ministers who delegated power to civil servants and a whole echelon of obedient soldiers, jailors, commandants, executioners, criminals and privileged prisoners. Pacifists had never envisaged such a Hell on earth nor had they realized that they bore some share of the guilt in its making.

NON-RESISTANCE DISCREDITED

This failure to resist, especially in the face of certain disaster and death, is now a potent factor in discussing our own responsibilities in the nuclear age. Non-resistance is wholly discredited for those at least who were the victims or the survivors of the terror. For example, it has been calculated that if the millions of the murdered had resisted arrest they would not have ended the terror but would have eliminated probably over a million murderers. Armed resistance to armed terror and not unarmed yielding has come out of this horrendous genocide known, wrongly, as the holocaust. The warning must be heeded. We can no longer envisage surrender as a responsible and ethically acceptable policy.

It is clearly impossible to return to the ethical foundations which prevailed before institutional terrorism became a tool of government. Hence an all-embracing pacifism cannot be acquitted and must be branded immoral, for it is an evil act which condones evil intentions. A policy in which a lamb is handed over to slaughter must be analyzed carefully. The analogy is taken from the butchery trade. It is legitimate for the farmer to sell the lamb to the wholesaler for it then to be passed on to the slaughter house. But if this analogy be applied to the national scale, where a population is condemned to death by its rulers, a semantic trick of criminal content confronts us. No one has the right to 'sacrifice' groups of human beings to naked power, to yield to terroristic threats on behalf of others. Appeasement is not only a farce but a sin.

Yet a return to belligerency is also excluded. The extreme cases of genocide, though fatal to straightforward pacifism and appeasement, set up norms of fear and preventive war which are as intolerable as unilateral measures of disarmament. Israel has experienced both the dire results of unarmed humiliation and extinction on the one hand, and of armed victory and supremacy without achieving a settlement and peace on the other. Either physical existence ceases or spiritual identity is lost. The present nuclear threshold of technology raises material and ethical issues which reopen the whole question of peace. Can peace be conceptualized at all? If so, can that state be achieved without humiliation?

Submission to the enemy is often portrayed on victory steles. The defeated, men, women, and children, are led away under the conqueror's yoke. The men will work as slaves until they drop, the women serve as concubines, and the children vanish in the slave markets. No one pretends that submission is pleasant or life-preserving. Hence the fear of defeat, and defeat itself, evoke elegies as eloquent as the tears of the sufferers. Our tradition is dominated by this deep-seated feeling which cries out against the fatal event when our identity is lost and all ends in disaster. The burning of Troy and the fall of Jerusalem symbolize this dread and act as a warning against the mental and physical conditions which cause the grief. The ruins of great cities stand as a constant reminder of the after-life of once great civilizations. Carthage, Rome, Ephesus, though rebuilt, still contain stones which tell the story of dissolution. Where rebuilding succeeds, plaques and shrines commemorate the writhing agony which preceded the cessation of hostilities. But the victors erect their statues of victory to demonstrate, as in the former Stalingrad, the supremacy of their arms. In submission there are two sides: the triumphant and the vanquished, and submission cannot be understood or accepted unless seen within the greater context.

The historical perspective is awe-inspiring. Both victory and defeat come to us not in prosaic terms only – as, say, reports in the books of Samuel or Greek historians – but in poetry. Not that Homer suppresses the horror of warfare; if there are embellishments, they serve to bring out the pathos of the Trojan war, the human foibles, the gods' malice, the terrible fate. But despite the universality of ultimate death and crumbling walls and treachery and fire in ships and palaces there does stand out the heroic. The heroes on both sides defend the honour of the city and the honour of the slighted.

The modern unilateralists simply do not comprehend the human need of pathos and honour. For them triumphalism has become a dirty concept. If Helen were stolen by the Trojans it would not concern them. Neither would they equip a fleet of Achaeans to sail to vindicate their cause, nor would they acknowledge their defeat if Helen stayed in Troy. A sacred cause, let alone a cause worthy of heroic resistance, is dismissed with a shrug. Not so in the Soviet Union nor among Islam radicals. The heroic tradition has become part of the propaganda of the state. The politburo has an imperium to defend, and it is an imperium which seeks to defeat such who have lost their belief in empire. The drums roll, the bugles call, the fanfares roar in the mighty conflict, now extended from Helen of Troy to class against class.

The advocacy of submission in the past occurred against a canvas of heroic action and actually took its stand within this tradition. Even in battle the fall of the hero retains pathos. A Hector who goes out to confront the formerly sulking Achilles knows in his heart that his last struggle will end in death. He submits to his fate, for it is his destiny. Nor does an Achilles remain blind to his own destiny. All alike submit to their mortality, for human life cannot transcend the boundaries of this submission. It pertains to the sadness of things that even the great and semi-divine succumb to their own demise. Heracles after his labours is tortured by the shirt of the defeated Nessus and welcomes death. Prometheus cannot escape from his rock. The ancient mythology pictures the givenness of power and human lack of strength.

If the hero must ultimately submit to fate he also achieves immortality for his cause. In the Biblical tradition Samson, a solar hero, vindicates himself in defeat. Until he is beguiled by Delilah he is only a braggart and hooligan; he becomes a divine instrument only in blindness and humiliation. His moment of triumph occurs when he is resolved to bring down the house of Dagon on himself and his enemies. In this final disaster he does not commit suicide but immolates himself for God. Here we have a glimpse on a small scale of how total disaster can be turned into triumph by active submission. No wonder Milton takes up the ancient story in his *Samson Agonistes*, for this fighter for freedom from chains becomes through poetry Milton's own symbol of triumph in blindness and defeat.

But the Samson spirit is also dangerous, for it may lead to fanaticism and a whole range of notions of irrational self-sacrifice through and for religious conviction. War becomes 'holy' in Judaism, Islam, and Christianity, not because it is necessarily fought for a good cause, but because a conflict is pronounced a Crusade or a *jihad* to stiffen morale and to justify unjustifiable aims. The Holy War appeals to reserves of heroic feeling without moral foundations. Thus Hitler's failing campaigns after 1942 were bolstered by open fanaticism and fear. It is against this unscrupulous exploitation of credulity that the prophetic protest against violence and war must be understood. Prophetic pacifism does not accept a holy war in an unholy context. Thus the prophets, who derived from and prospered in a military milieu (such as Elisha's), insist on submission to God, to a righteous cause and judgement.

ENIGMATIC CROSSROADS

We have reached an enigmatic crossroads in the argument. According to the prophetic tradition, conflicts have to be tested as to their rightness. Hence a relative value judgement is inevitably introduced of who is to judge what is right and wrong? When is a conflict to be ended by simply giving in? Are there no causes worthy of defence and must all swords be turned into ploughshares, all guns into butter, all nuclear missiles into third-world aids? Does submission come to mean the exact opposite to the Islamic concept of Islam, namely submission to Allah? Can there be a substitute to Allah, so that rightful submission can be demanded in favour of an aggressor?

The prophetic tradition of the Old Testament cannot give a simple answer. On the one hand you have the passion for peace, but on the other hand you also have a militant enthusiasm for righteousness. The defence of the poor and defenceless does not advocate submission but rather resistance. Even the defence of Jerusalem becomes legitimate at the time of Isaiah. The oracles against the foreign nations are inspired by a sort of utopian Zionism in which Assyria, Egypt, Ethiopia, Babylon and others submit to Zion, and not the other way round. Only when Jerusalem becomes corrupt and is not worth defending her destiny must be destruction, misery, and exile. Jeremiah at the end of the kingdom concludes that capitulation to Babylon is morally justified and even necessary.

An extraordinary shift of interest now occurs. The centre of gravity moves from the exiles and those who sing with despair the songs of Zion in Babylon, longing for vengeance, to Jeremiah himself. Accused of treachery he is martyred and vindicated. Jeremiah becomes the personified and concrete type of submission. It is Jeremiah who sees himself in the sacrificial role of a lamb led to the slaughter. Before the expression becomes a stereotyped cliché Jeremiah fulfils the role uniquely. He is not defeated in submitting himself to despair. He is not dishonoured by advocating capitulation to Babylon. His witness is to the truth, that is to events as they will take place, to the pattern of things in the natural world, to the power which rules and divides. In this way Jeremiah submits himself to his God and to no human agency. Yet his role as the Lamb led to the slaughter is not vaguely mystical, for he identifies with his people as a man of tears. His suffering is the price he pays for his role as prophet, as an interpreter of the times.

The shift is to be apprehended in the extreme personalization. We should no longer speak of submission, in the abstract and neutral voice, but of the martyr, the witness, the servant, who gives his life and work for the truth. Instead of submitting to the power he submits himself to the only true power. The struggle is moral and spiritual and it is crowned with success, for though the earthly power would erase the words, annul the record, the prophet perpetuates his martyrdom by the written word and the handing on of the words in a community of disciples.

In the Biblical tradition Jeremiah does not stand alone. During the exile itself and subsequently after the return, the figure of the unnamed servant extends the role of the victorious, kingly, triumphant Israel, which in submitting to God suffers, endures, expiates sin, restores and heals the wounds. The picture remains highly paradoxical, for the servant is humiliated, disfigured, scorned, tortured, killed, and buried, and through tasting the uttermost horror of isolation and abandonment he becomes the acceptable sacrifice, the pure soul which is given and gives for the outrages committed by the foe. How is this done? Certainly not by revenge and slaughter, but by an inward essence of humanity, by an ontological and indestructible goodness which *serves*. Thus the passivity of the lamb, which does not open its mouth and is led to the slaughter, actively releases energies which create and redeem. Peace and perfection are achieved miraculously, and not politically.

The servant ideology is tested again and again in community. It is by no means the only prevalent ideology, for the world goes on in its brutal course of oppression and disaster. Thus the author of the book of Job universalizes the problem of undeserved suffering against a cosmic canvas of indifference. To whom can Job submit, to whom ought he to submit? He is no lamb led to the slaughter, but a lion exposed to the nothingness of the void. Should he submit to nature? To moralizing friends? To the hindering Satan? To a matter of fact wife? He will not submit until the account can be straightened out and settled. The truth lies in the search for God to whom alone one may submit.

Submission seems to become a highly individualized affair of the spirit. But the appearance is misleading, for Job may reflect the experience of Israel in exile. Hence despite the pain there is hope and restitution at the end. To submit to God is not a negative concept. This is stressed even more clearly in the *Aqeda*, the tantalizing story of Abraham and Isaac. This account, so briefly, rendered in Genesis chapter 22, may belong to some pre-exilic period, but whatever its origins it becomes an interpretation of the inexplicable ordeal of Israel. Both father and son submit to the savage demand that the former offer the latter. It may well be that the angelic intervention 'Do not!' changes the whole tone of this appalling need to sacrifice and that it constitutes a prohibition directed against heathen practices of infanticide. Nevertheless, a purely didactic interpretation of this kind, which replaces humanistic ethics for divine authority, misses the point. A lamb caught by its horns in the thicket and slaughtered symbolizes the substitution that must take place. Obedience to the law does not rescind the absolute nature of the demand: obedience is better than sacrifice.

Thus the *Aqeda* became, and remains, the challenge of submission in faith. An endless stream of comment follows the Biblical story which evoke levels of fear and trembling. Death is never far away, and there is even a lingering tradition that the boy was killed and resurrected, that both father and son underwent the ordeal. The writer of the Epistle to the Hebrews exploits this tradition: 'By faith Abraham, when he was tried, offered up Isaac . . . accounting that God as able to raise him up, even from the dead'. The typology applies to Christ and the Christian.

In this manner a strong ritual of submission became linked with the Passover. The remembrance of the Exodus from Egypt and the redemption of the servant Israel after and through the submission to God became enshrined in the domestic and public festival. The sharing of the bread, the communion of the cup of wine, and the eating of the lamb were the outward and joyful acts of the strange conviction that submission leads to triumph, to victory and salvation. Christians inherited this tradition through their Messiah, Jesus who before he suffered took bread and wine and gave his life as the lamb of God. The meal became a celebration of victory because he who submitted to humiliation and death was raised by God in triumph. This is the cornerstone of the Christian preaching and the confession of the eucharistic faith.

Texts and words and liturgies reflect the life of the community. They may also conceal the insoluble problems of life. Both Jews and Christians have a long history of conflict in which Passover and Eucharist stand over against the actual events, where either the policy of submission was not tried, or when tried failed. A consistent agreement of ideology and policy only rarely succeeded. In other words, a total and uncompromising pacifism floundered in the ocean of persecutions. A distinction forced itself upon communities and individuals: namely, to submit to God is right, even if it leads to defeat and death, but to submit to the enemy is wrong, lest tyranny and falsehood triumph in God's world. This distinction is sharp as a razor: loyalty to the one God and fidelity to the community and a 'good confession', a refusal to betray and to be enticed by rewards, pertain to a submission to God and not to man.

These general principles are fleshed out in the New Testament both in the person of Jesus and in the witness of the Apostolic Church. It is axiomatic to hold up the Christ as an example of non-violence, and out of context a picture of the pacific teacher can be obtained whose special counsel of perfection extends to the miraculous: do not resist evil, love your enemies, give, forgive, love those who hate you. But it is easily forgotten that this perfectionism rests upon the divinity of Jesus, his sonship of the Father, his fulfilment of the Aqeda tradition as the cosmic lamb who takes away the sins of the world, who substitutes his eternal self for the passing world which he conquers. This is not non-violence or pacifism *tout court*, but the royal conquest of the Lion of Judah. Hence the same Christ who submits to the traitor Judas, to the Sanhedrin, to the High Priest, to Pilate, and to the soldiers does not submit to *them* but through them to the Father. The truth is inviolate, the life unbroken, the Son glorified.

This witness to the truth is openly shown in the works of Christ during the brief ministry on earth. This ministry is aggressive and openly hostile to the traditions of man. Jesus is 'submissive' to a certain extent: to his parents as a boy and young man, to the law, even to Rome. He does not meddle with the occupying power, nor with the system of exploitation. The Kingdom of God and the power which he manifests *transcend* the political realm, but in healing the sick and in exorcizing demons Jesus confronts the destructive evil in the human race. The faith which he evokes and demands is the very opposite of a compromise with evil or a submission to pragmatic considerations. His war is a campaign, a strategic and rational assault upon the chaos around him.

APOSTOLIC PARADOX

The Apostolic Church lives by this Gospel which modern analysts may well call a dialectical attitude to life. On the one hand the chosen band of disciples forswears violence and is not touched by military and political events, shows its loyalty to the powers that be by paying tribute and by dissociating itself from revolutionary armed activity; on the other the missionary activity, first in Judaea, then in Samaria, and soon in the Greek speaking world, until even Rome is reached, proclaims Christ as a way of life, as an abolition of the old and the fulfilment of the new. Neither Peter nor Paul nor the ordinary Christians strike us as 'lambs', in the sense in which Nietzsche and his followers understood and loathed the religion of the pale Nazarene. They are truly men and women who stand up for their faith and will not submit to be silenced or to restrict their sacred work.

It would be invidious to quote from the Acts and the Epistles to bring out the fine nuances of resistance and submissiveness. No doubt the early Christians saw themselves, as Paul says, as scorned, despised, treated as the scum, as lambs among wolves, as sheep around their shepherd. They did not resist by force of arms, but they knew themselves to be engaged in a war of apocalyptic dimensions. One need not turn to the book of Revelation to be persuaded that humanistic pacifism is as far from their place in the world as a submission to lies. Martyrs to the truth cannot expect peace on earth. Yet in this fellowship of suffering – as Paul in prison, stoned, shipwrecked, beaten etc. – sanity prevails, excesses are to be avoided, life is to be lived fully, and institutions are to be protected

Perhaps the subtlest presentation of the paradox meets the reader in I Peter. One wonders how the writer and the recipients, whom we cannot locate with any certainty, envisage their daily lamb-like existence in the empire. They acknowledge the power of emperor and magistrate, of law and order, even if oppressive; they would carry on their perfectionist lives in subjection to this order because they acknowledge God as the sole author of cosmic life and government. The most radical view is taken of martyrdom as a Christ-like witness not only to good but also to wicked powers. The tone of the exhortation is to the community, but individuals are expected to heed the counsel of perfection. The context is still eschatological. Hence the demonic onslaughts can be endured because the end is in sight. This end is not death but eternal life. Just as the slaughtered Lamb is enthroned as the shepherd of souls so the souls of the martyrs will be transformed into his likeness.

In this extraordinary way the Holy War continued and continues to the present day in a strategy of physical endurance and spiritual resistance. Never is there a thought of capitulation or treason, even when there is every reason to yield to superior power and beguiling blackmail. Nor is the Christian stance entirely scriptural or sectarian. The immense legacy of Greek thinking and feeling flows like a tributary into the Christian tradition, though it is not always acknowledged. True, some Greek schools of thought would support a secular utilitarianism, a yielding of principles to 'Eat and drink, for tomorrow we die'. But a cynical or epicurean or materialistic ethic has never blended with Christian vocation and duty.

Athens and Jerusalem are the two pillars of our stand against tyranny and self-pleasing decadence. The tragedy of Antigone, written by Sophocles and performed at c. 430 BC, enshrines the principle of resistance even in the face of certain disaster. Antigone insists on the burial of her brother Polynices slain by his brother Eteocles in their fratricidal battle; her uncle Creon, the new king, summons a council of elders and promulgates his decree, allegedly for the security of the polis, that the corpse is to lie unattended to rot. Creon speaks of his office, thinks of himself, and makes absolute demands. For Antigone they are unacceptable, just as he as a tyrant is also an enemy. The Gods, the laws of kinship, the spirit of the deceased, demand burial. The conflict cannot be avoided, even if her sister favours some sort of compromise. We move, as do the principal actors, in a world of relative values, of possible rewards at the expense of honour. Antigone is not a perfect girl; she also through her passion for her cause is caught as a flawed heroine by the ambiguities of the case. Without her passion, however, and with a weakened conviction and less courage she would not act and conquer the brutality of the hated tyrant. She is not a lamb in the Christian sense, but she is a martyr to a transcendentally true cause. The pathos of her ordeal derives from that cause. She who would prefer life to death, even marriage to barren virginity, confronts the powerful, having made the great decision. She is carried off to be walled up, the virgin bride of death. But Creon scores no victory: his wife and son commit suicide and he 'enjoys' the total void of himself.

This heroine of a tomb-prison blocked with rocks may seem remote from our nuclear age, but Antigone came to life as a symbol during the war against the Nazis. This drama, as personal in its individualism as anything in the Bible, portrayed the inner and outer conflict: how and when should I resist tyranny? Christians may not respond to the tragic pathos, having been conditioned to an optimistic climate, yet the present circumstances of either–or may force them to re-enter the tragic necessity. And even if they discount the pathos and would opt for a more serene and philosophical choice they can hardly ignore Socrates, who less than a century after Sophocles refused to leave Athens and to conform to his enemies' ultimatum. The hemlock which he drank with such happy ease also stands for a legitimate act of resistance, a spiritual victory over brute force and foolish arrogance. Even if less detached from the world, many men and women of goodwill must be guided, like the Stoics, not by emotion but by a simple and soldierly sense of duty. These examples of antiquity are not out of date. They lack the Biblical imagery, the extremes of lamb-like submission and the majesty of the Lion of Judah, of crucifixion and resurrection, but in an irreligious age, in a post-Christian society the voice of Athens as of an enlightened humanism also must be heard.

The theme is too complex to be reduced to a simple equation. The Lamb that was slain and now reigns is not a symbol that can be directly applied to military and political issues. The only thing that can be concluded without equivocation is negative: the Christian and Western civilization cannot be abandoned to savage and irreversible tyranny. To submit there is to betray the truth. To invite the foe in the hope of an easy accommodation is not only unheroic but apostasy.

But this reduction of our theme to a negative formula will not do. The *lamb led to the slaughter* stands firm as a symbol of positive faith. Its idealism is the very negation of nihilism and despair. The separating of this symbol from what it symbolizes is an act of deception. Far from easing us into submitting to lies the heroic role of self-surrender can only be justified in the cause of the Kingdom of God. The lamb stands against 'Christian Buddhism' and for the reality of God in his cosmic and eternal Being. Hence submission is not a political or military option, but part of an immense edifice. Atheism and materialism are the enemies of this order of indestructible truth; no one knew this better than Marx, Lenin, Stalin as well as Hitler and his gangsters. To submit to their heirs is to deny the divine order, but to sacrifice everything for the truth is to defy their cruel nihilism.

This apocalyptic confrontation ends not in defeat but in ideological victory: the Lamb is slain, the Lamb is enthroned. Even in these days of anguish we may derive solace from the promise of immortality and resurrection. Goethe was not a confessing Christian, but I love his words which his friends inscribed in the great hall of his house at the time of his death:

'Death's image, though so moving to the heart,
  Calls up no terror in a wise man's breast,
  But urges back to living and to action.
  Nor to the pious does it spell the end
  But fortifies by hope to reach salvation.'

7
WHERE DOES THE NUCLEAR-FREE PATH LEAD?

Hugh Beach

7. Where does the nuclear-free path lead?

THE PRACTICAL AND ETHICAL CONSEQUENCES OF A NUCLEAR FREE BRITAIN

The Church and the Bomb is a cautious and pragmatic document, not without logical difficulties. Since, in the authors' view, 'a nuclear component in deterrence is not sufficiently compelling to outweigh the huge moral imperatives against using nuclear weapons at all', they conclude that a Christian must 'decide against it and risk the political and human consequences of blackmail and defeat by someone with fewer moral inhibitions.'[1] On this basis, as one of the authors has recognized, 'logic might have demanded an immediate root and branch nuclear pacifist solution'.[2] Indeed it is difficult to see how logic could have demanded otherwise. The report, however, balances this judgement with an equally explicit recognition that 'total abandonment of nuclear weapons by one of the alliances in the international line-up could undoubtedly have serious destabilizing effects. As a policy option . . . it lies in the realms of fantasy as things are at present'.[3] Consequently the practical actions which the report recommends are at best a tiny step towards what it regards as the Christian position. 'For the United Kingdom to adopt a policy which marginally reduced the nuclear weaponry of the NATO alliance might therefore, in our judgement, actually increase security and at the same time create an initiative which might well lead to a positive move from others'.[4]

The policy in question is, of course, unilateral nuclear renunciation by the United Kingdom. Logic might have demanded as much from any country possessing or relying on nuclear weapons: France for example, or the Federal German Republic. (The report describes the latter country as a non-nuclear weapon state.[5] Nevertheless it harbours the highest concentration of nuclear warheads in Western Europe – of which more later.)

But this narrow interpretation of unilateralism also stems from a pragmatic recognition that if the same prescription were applied more widely, to all the European members of NATO for example, it would infallibly lead to the break-up of the alliance; and this is not desired. What the report recommends therefore is 'renunciation by Britain . . . combined if humanly possible with continued membership of NATO'. 'Withdrawal from all alliances . . . because it might be seen by (the USSR) as a possible beginning of a break-up of NATO could well not have the creative effect on negotiations of a unilateral gesture within the framework of NATO itself, and might indeed prove merely destructive'.[6] So what the authors propose is a number of 'carefully phased steps of unilateral disarmament by Britain, within the NATO framework, which we believe will have no destabilizing effect but, in conjunction with other confidence building measures, may facilitate the multilateral disarmament negotiations of the super powers'.[7]

In thus preferring pragmatism to logic the report takes what is not only a typically British line, but also a rational one. There is no solution to the nuclear problem which is free from paradoxes, and the report itself sets out several of them.[8] The 'carefully phased steps' which the report proposes have one sovereign virtue compared with much that passes for theological thinking. Since they are all feasible – indeed one of the principal political parties in Britain appears to have committed itself to a very similar programme – it follows that there is at least the possibility of proof – or disproof. If Britain were to act as the report proposes, and the desired consequences were to follow: namely that a boost was given to the disarmament negotiations of the superpowers without destabilizing side effects, then the report would have been vindicated. If, contrariwise, there was no effect upon the disarmament policies of the superpowers but a demonstrable degree of destabilization – say in the form of disarray within NATO – the report would have been proved quite simply wrong. Canon Oestreicher makes this pragmatism explicit. 'Would we,' he asks 'maintain our qualified unilateralism if we were persuaded that this would make a nuclear war more likely? Of course not. But we are not so persuaded. We believe and argue this in some detail – that the calculated risk of taking significant unilateral steps may help to break the multilateral logjam. We believe this to be much less dangerous than present policies'.[9] In short, there are two touchstones by which the report seeks to be judged: first, that the policies that it recommends should lead to increased security (or at worst, no destabilization); secondly that they should give a fillip to the disarmament negotiations of the superpowers. Consequently, whatever may be thought of the underlying theological judgements, it is by criteria in the field of defence policy and diplomacy that the practical action recommended by the report stands or falls.

The substantive recommendations of the report[10] deal with two distinct topics. The first is renunciation by the United Kingdom of its 'independent nuclear deterrent'. By this is meant the Polaris missile and submarines (including work on Chevaline) and the intention to acquire Trident. The second is withdrawal from 'other nuclear weapons', of British or US manufacture, whether held by or for British units, or on British soil. It is the contention of this chapter that the authors of the report may well be right in their judgement on the first topic, but are quite certainly and very dangerously wrong on the second.

Britain's 'independent nuclear deterrent', as it now exists, is the outcome of the Nassau agreement signed by Kennedy and Macmillan on 21 December 1962. Under this agreement the Americans supplied Polaris missiles and related equipment (effectively the centre sections of the boats) for four submarines, and promised continuing spares supply and maintenance support – not least the supply of the U-235 fissile material. The submarines and warheads were designed and built in Britain. The force is wholly owned by the United Kingdom, and responsibility for its operational use rests with the British Government alone. The force is committed to NATO and targetted in accordance with alliance policy and concepts under plans made by the Supreme Commander, 'except where her Majesty's Government may decide that supreme national interests are at stake'. Each of the submarines contains sixteen missiles. Originally each missile carried a single warhead, but they were modified some years ago to carry three smaller warheads (each of 200 kiloton yield) which become slightly spread out during the re-entry phase so that the target is well straddled. This is of value against cities or other large targets. More recently, British Governments of both political persuasions have put in hand a further modification programme for the warheads, codenamed Chevaline, said to be

113

in response to Soviet anti-ballistic missile developments (which exist only around Moscow). Chevaline includes advanced penetration aids and a manoeuvrable payload. Development is now substantially complete, and is expected to maintain the effectiveness of the Polaris system into the early 1990s.

The resulting system is of staggering cost-effectiveness. Since 1969 there has always been one boat on patrol and ready to fire – carrying more explosive power than all the munitions used in World War II put together. The Soviet Union is said never to have found one of these boats on patrol.[11] In 1981–82 the nuclear strategic force cost only 2.2 per cent of the defence budget, or about 0.1 per cent of GNP – a small figure even by comparison with what the Government spends on foreign aid. During the late 1960s and 1970s this force attracted little or no public notice, and a degree of concern that reflected less its capability than its cost.

Matters changed however, with the announcement on 15 July 1980, that the Government planned to replace the Polaris fleet with the Trident system[12] acquired from the United States Government on similar terms to its predecessor. It is an immensely more capable system. As operated presently by the United States (the C–4 system) the missile has almost twice the range of Polaris (4000 nautical miles, compared to 2,500) and each carries eight independently targetted warheads. The British, however, will acquire a later system (D–5) now being developed by the Americans for deployment in 1989. It will be significantly larger, and able either to carry the same payload a much greater distance and with greater accuracy, or to carry still more warheads over approximately the same range. It is also correspondingly more expensive. On the Government estimates, the cost of the whole D–5 system will be some 7.5 million at 1981 prices. At its peak, around 1990, Trident will consume 6 per cent of the defence budget and nearly 12 per cent of the equipment budget.

In technical terms the aim of the Trident system has been defined as 'posing a convincing threat of inflicting on key aspects of Soviet State Power damage which any Soviet leadership would regard as out of all proportion to any likely gain from aggression against us'.[13] If this is shorthand for the ability to obliterate Moscow it seems to represent no change in policy. The price, however, is much higher, and this has prompted a restatement of its political significance. In earlier years much was made of the 'top table' argument, whereby an independent strategic nuclear capability was seen as the price of access to deliberations of ultimate significance in the field of peace and war.

SECOND CENTRE

The deliberate exclusion of the United Kingdom from talks on Strategic Arms Limitation (SALT), Strategic Arms Reduction (START) and Intermediate Nuclear Force (INF) have shown up the limitations of that. The case of Trident as it is now made, is based upon the concept of a 'second centre of decision' within NATO.[14] 'A Soviet leadership . . . might believe that it could impose its will on Europe, by military force, without becoming involved in strategic nuclear war with the United States'. A nuclear decision by the United Kingdom 'would be the decision of a separate and independent power whose survival in freedom would be directly and immediately threatened by aggression in Europe . . . An adversary assessing the consequences of possible aggression in Europe would have to regard a Western defence containing these powerful independent elements as a harder one to predict and a more dangerous one to assail than one in which nuclear retaliatory power rested in United States hands alone'.[15]

There are several difficulties with this argument. The first is that no-one has yet succeeded (indeed there has been notably few attempts) to define circumstances in which it could conceivably make sense for the United Kingdom to use its Polaris/ Trident force when the United States was unprepared to do so. Such use, by a country which presents an almost unique concentration of cities and industries, unprotected by any but the flimsiest of civil defence provision, against any potential assailant with nuclear weapons, would be blatantly suicidal. The credibility of such use, solo, against a Soviet leadership that was doing no more than seeking to impose its will on Europe by military force is low to vanishing. As *The Church and the Bomb* points out, to pose so unreal a threat is arguably at least as dangerous to this country as to any Soviet leadership, and possibly even more dangerous to the USA if it is seen as a means of triggering an otherwise reluctant administration into using its own strategic forces. McNamara's famous indictment of limited nuclear capabilities operating independently as 'dangerous, expensive, prone to obsolescence and lacking in credibility as a deterrent'[16] would fit the case precisely.

The residual truth in the 'second centre' argument is this: that an independent capability to obliterate Moscow is credible as a deterrent against one threat only and that is the threat of a direct nuclear attack upon the United Kingdom itself. We consider later whether there are not preferable means of deterring this threat (to the extent that it exists at all) rather than one that rests upon making this country 'harder to predict and more dangerous to assail'.

There are of course darker reasons for a British Government to opt for Polaris/Trident. One is as an insurance against NATO breaking up. This prompts the reflection that the same premium might be better invested in measures designed to prevent this happening rather than securing against it. It is, of course, true that the British decision to maintain Polaris and to acquire Trident has been welcomed publicly by President Reagan (as major partner in the deal he could hardly do otherwise), and its importance recognized by other members of the alliance. But this is not to say that a decision on the part of the United Kingdom to phase out its strategic forces would be destabilizing to the alliance if it were done for good and sufficient reasons. In this respect *The Church and the Bomb* is probably right – provided that renunciation was undertaken not as part of a 'root and branch' rejection of alliance nuclear policy but as a prudent reinvestment of scarce resources.[17]

On this point also, official arguments are less than convincing. 'Those who argue that expenditure on Trident would be better devoted to strengthening our conventional forces must consider whether future Soviet leaders are more likely to be deterred by an invulnerable second strike submarine launched ballistic missile force, or for example, two additional armoured divisions with 300 extra tanks (even if this were a sensible alternative) given that the Warsaw Pact already outnumbers NATO in tanks by some 30,000'.[18] As stated this alternative is, of course, not sensible; nor is there space here to argue the financial case in full. But it is indisputably true that even on the Government's own assumption of 3 per cent real growth in defence expenditure until the mid 1980s, the pressure of rising equipment costs will compel further reductions in front line conventional forces well before the end of the 1980s. The true choice, therefore, if we take the same example, is between abandoning Trident; or withdrawing and disbanding two of the existing armoured divisions in the British Army of the Rhine – of which in any case there are to be only three, and they but partially equipped with the most modern tanks, guns and armoured personnel carriers. Put in this way the argument about alliance stability looks very different.

Nor is it helpful to look at this problem, as government spokesmen sometimes do, from the point of view of what the Soviet Union would most fear. The object of a sane defence policy is not to instil fear into a political adversary as an end in itself, but rather to reduce the likelihood of war. The true guarantee of peace and freedom for this country, as for Western Europe as a whole, lies in the coherence, self confidence and self respect of the countries of Western Europe underpinned by the Atlantic Alliance. This is the pearl of great price, and the report is at least entitled to argue that this cause would be better served by maintaining a robust conventional contribution on the part of the United Kingdom, rather than by retaining outdated independent strategic pretensions.

Which brings us to the last and darkest, but probably the most fundamental reason why successive governments ever since World War II have sought and maintained an independent British strategic nuclear capability: they have seen it as vital to Britain's self esteem. In France this function of nuclear forces has always been both central and acknowledged. In the United Kingdom it lurks between the lines, and this is a pity, because the motive in itself is not ignoble. It is only a slight caricature to say that Polaris, having almost no possible military function, serves as a comparable prestige symbol to that of a loss-making national airline (the cost to the taxpayer being roughly equivalent – as is the degree of reliance on American technology). If this were acknowledged more openly it would permit a rational debate on the second major ground for renunciation urged by *The Church and the Bomb* – namely that it might well lead to 'positive moves from others'.

UNILATERALISM UNREALISTIC

Certainly throughout the negotiation of the Non-Proliferation Treaty most non-nuclear states held that their renunciation of

117

nuclear weapons should be accompanied by a commitment on the part of the nuclear powers to reduce their nuclear arsenals.[19] Since the Treaty came into force thirteen years ago no nuclear power has in fact done so. It is arguable, therefore, that the renunciation of a national capability by one of the founder nuclear states would have a symbolic influence out of all proportion to its real importance. Most of the British arguments for retaining an independent capability could apply, *mutatis mutandis*, to other potential owners, and the British Polaris/Trident force is thus a tacit charter for proliferators.

This argument, however, represents a triumph of hope over experience. The overwhelming likelihood is that other nations will continue to do what they always have done, and that is to take their decision of high policy on the basis of what they consider to be their own national interest. The notion that they would be shamed into following us is sentimental not to say sanctimonious. Historical precedents tell in exactly the other direction – chemical warfare being a case in point. The UK renounced an offensive capability 25 years ago, and since then has seen the Soviet offensive capability more than double. Gesture having proved wholly inappropriate to this type of issue, it is plain that there is no substitute for hard bargaining, as the UK Government has increasingly recognized in recent years.[20] As in the chemical field, so in the nuclear; the prospects for progress are best served not by gesture, however spectacular, taken outside the negotiating process, but by hard headed bargaining within it. And the time for this is now uniquely propitious.

The United States and the Soviet Union are now engaged in discussions at Geneva covering the full spectrum of 'strategic' and 'intermediate' nuclear forces: that is all but the shortest range 'battlefield' artillery and missile systems. The United States' opening bid is for a reduction by one third of strategic missile warheads, and a 'zero option' for intermediate missile systems. If these aims, or anything approaching them could be secured this would indeed 'actually increase security and at the same time create an initiative which might well lead to positive moves from others'. This situation is unprecedented, and it would be shortsighted in the extreme to allow a general disillusionment with past progress in bilateral discussions to blunt the will for progress now. In the strategic talks the British (and French) nuclear forces are not on the agenda. But there is no logic in their exclusion from the intermediate nuclear force negotiations, and the USSR has pressed, from the beginning, for their inclusion. More recently the Soviet leader has explicitly proposed a direct equation between the size of the Soviet European medium range missile forces and those deployed by Britain and France. 'If the number of British and French missiles were scaled down the number of Soviet ones would be additionally reduced by as many'. This Mr Andropov described as 'a really honest zero option'.[21] Admittedly the terms on which he did so, namely the abandonment by NATO of the planned deployment of Cruise Missiles and Pershing II, makes the bargain as it stands unattractive, for reasons discussed below. But the principle of including the British forces in these negotiations, though stoutly resisted by British officials, is beyond all question logical.

It follows that in proposing the unilateral renunciation of the Polaris/Trident force the authors of *The Church and the Bomb* have missed a great opportunity – even by their own standards. If it be granted, as seems most likely, that the marginal military significance of the British strategic force, coupled with its high opportunity cost in the NATO context, makes the successful completion of the Trident programme highly problematical, it follows that much the best course of action would be to obtain the highest price for its abandonment within the context of the bilateral negotiation. Had they suggested this, rather than the theatrical gesture of unilateral renunciation, it could indeed have become '*a unilateral stage within a multilateral process*'.[22]

CRUISE

We turn next to the question of the American Intermediate Range systems stationed in the United Kingdom. For the last fifteen years these have consisted of a force of about 160 F111 aircraft stationed in bases in East Anglia. They are wholly owned and controlled by the United States Government but their use, in an emergency, would be a matter for joint decision between the two governments in the light of circumstances prevailing at the time. These aircraft have a combat radius (with average payload, unrefuelled) of about 1,000 nautical miles – but it is usually assumed that they can carry nuclear weapons into the USSR and are tasked to do so. These are swing-winged supersonic aircraft (Mach 2.2) designed to approach at high altitude and then penetrate at low level as a precaution against air defence. Each can carry two nuclear warheads; but when regard is had to operational factors such as serviceability, survivability, reliability and penetration, the proportion of deliverable warheads is assessed at less than 15 per cent.[23] Thus, as a system, it is approaching obsolescence.

It is therefore planned to replace these aircraft, starting this year (1983), with a similar number (160) of Tomahawk Cruise Missiles. These are low flying, air breathing missiles using a self-correcting internal guidance system and have much in common with unmanned aircraft, although only about twelve feet long. They each carry a single nuclear warhead but their ability to penetrate is high, since they fly below 250 feet directed by a guidance system whereby a computer compares the ground over which they are flying with a map stored in their memory. With a range of some 1,500 miles they have the capability to reach Moscow (just) but would take about three hours to do so. The launchers are highly mobile, and in time of tension would be quickly and widely concealed away from their normal bases. This will be practised in peace time, though naturally without live warheads or fuelled missiles. Once so dispersed they will be virtually impossible to locate and attack, and it will, of course, be quite pointless to strike the places that they have left.

Almost every propaganda point made against these missiles by the protestors of Greenham Common is therefore wrong. With their slow time of flight and small numbers they are utterly inappropriate for a disarming attack against the Soviet Union, let alone a 'first strike'. Consequently to categorize them as war-fighting weapons is incorrect: they are essentially weapons of deterrence. Unlike the F111 aircraft which are tied to fixed bases, the Tomahawks once dispersed constitute absolutely no temptation to the Russians to pre-empt. They come as close as is possible for a land base system to providing an invulnerable second strike capability – as arms control theory would prescribe. The cost of their development and production is being met entirely by the United States; and although the bases will largely be paid for from NATO Infrastructure Funds the total cost of the UK share will be no more than £16 million (at 1980 prices). The UK manpower requirement is equally low: 220 persons as a contribution to security guards.[24] Assuming, therefore, that there is a need for such a system, cruise missiles have many advantages from the UK point of view.

But when it comes to providing a rationale for their deployment, neither the United Kingdom Government nor the NATO Governments at large have carried conviction. From the UK viewpoint it is a misfortune that this project, being essentially a one for one replacement of an ageing and vulnerable manned aircraft with an up-to-date and relatively invulnerable unmanned craft, should form part of a much wider programme with quite different characteristics. This wider programme caters for the installation of a further 464 Tomahawks in the Federal Republic of Germany, Holland, Belgium and Italy – in all of which they will represent a totally novel capability – and for the replacement of the 108 Pershing I missils in United States ownership in Western Germany, by the same number of Pershing II missiles. The latter would be the first ground based ballistic missile in Western Europe with a range in excess of 500 miles and thus capable of striking targets well within the Soviet Union (though not Moscow). Its time of flight is only fifteen minutes – consequently the Russians could have as little as ten minutes' warning or less. It is highly accurate and highly destructive.[25] As such, it certainly has many of the characteristics of a first strike weapon.

It is even more unfortunate that this programme, in its entirety, has become inextricably linked both in public presentation and in diplomacy with the Soviet deployment of the SS–20 missile system. The latter is, indeed, a formidable threat. The missile has a range of 3,000 miles, which means that it could hit anywhere in Europe (but not, of course, the USA) from Russian soil. Even if placed East of the Urals it could hit every European capital except Lisbon. Each missile can carry three warheads. Some 330 are reported to have been deployed since 1977, and production continues. It is assumed that about one-third are targetted on China, the remainder on Europe. This would make over 600 warheads even without reload.

But the linkage of NATO's Tomahawk/Pershing II programme with the deployment of SS–20 is doubly misleading. In the first place SS–20 does not represent a novel threat in kind. Since the early 1960s the Russians have had some 600 missile systems deployed in Russia, with ranges such that they can cover the whole of Europe but not the United States of America. The number of these missiles is being reduced as SS–20 is deployed[26] and there is substance in the Soviet claim that this changeover represents no more than technical modernization of the system.[27] By contrast the Tomahawks and Pershing II are a threat to the Soviet homeland, from land based missiles in Europe, of a kind that has not existed before and must appear in Soviet eyes as an exact parallel, in terms of provocation, to the famous Soviet missiles in Cuba of the early 1960s.

The second reason why it is misleading to speak of the Tomahawk/Pershing II programme as the counter to the SS–20 is that this cannot be their operational role. The SS–20 is mobile and can be transported on heavy wheeled launchers; consequently, once dispersed, it no longer constitutes a feasible target. The targets for Tomahawk and Pershing II will be air bases in Western Russia, lines of communication, control centres and other military bases and reserves.[28] From the point of view of a strictly military calculus these targets are essential – but a number of questions remain. For example, would not so called American Central Systems suffice: namely the 400 Poseidon warheads which are assumed to be available to SACEUR for NATO targeting?[29] Does it in any case make sense to plan for the discharge of nuclear weapons in such vast numbers into Western Russia, in pursuit of tactical objectives, when such use must infallibly trigger strategic systems on both sides? More pertinently still, since the technology will shortly become available for the highly effective attack of Warsaw Pact Main Operating Bases, and fixed lines of communication, by non-nuclear means, should not that be the main thrust of development? It would then be possible for NATO to avow the true function and purpose of these missiles, which is purely deterrent. They provide the means to threaten retaliation against the use of any nuclear systems by Russia, in Europe, and to hold at risk Soviet forces in depth thus enforcing dispersal and so enhancing NATO's conventional capability to defend.

Meanwhile the fact must be faced that in the public mind, and by deliberate act of NATO governments, the NATO modernization plan for deployment of Tomahawk and Pershing II has become inextricably linked with the SS–20. By formal decision of the alliance, on 12 December 1979, it was agreed both to pursue the modernization programme, and that the USA would undertake simultaneously to begin negotiations with the USSR about limiting land based long range theatre nuclear forces.[30] From this decision, though not without further prompting, has sprung the INF negotiation, the 'zero option', and the Andropov offer described above. The NATO decision has thus assumed a political significance out of all proportion to its original function; it has become a symbol of the unity and effective working of the Atlantic Alliance and the role of Europe between the superpowers. In American eyes it has become a battle for the soul of Europe.[31] And in this there is at least some sense, because politically the significance of these missiles is exactly the reverse of what hostile publicity has proposed. The contention that they represent an effort, on the part of the United States, to confine any future nuclear conflict to Europe is self evidently false. In fact they represent the implantation, upon European soil, of what is functionally a US central system (i.e. with the ability to strike Russia). This is an unmistakable token – if any were needed beyond the 500,000 American men, women and children already stationed in Western Germany – of the inextricable involvement of the continental United States in any European war, which is the true heart of deterrence.

So whether we like it or not, the programme for deployment of Tomahawks in the UK in simple replacement of the F111 – which has much to commend it from the point of view of the UK – has been overlaid in significance by the NATO programme of which it forms a part. The hard facts are that to press on steadfastly with the NATO programme has become, at one and the same time, both a highly important token of NATO solidarity, and the best chance of inducing a favourable outcome to the INF talks. Contrariwise, for the UK to withdraw from the programme at this stage, as *The Church and the Bomb* proposes,[32] would be calculated both to destabilize NATO, and to abort the most promising discussions in the whole field of disarmament; the forum within which the eventual British withdrawal from its strategic nuclear capability could most logically and profitably be pursued. It thus fails utterly to measure up to the criteria proposed by the authors of the report: namely, having *no* destabilizing effect, and *facilitating* the multilateral disarmament regotiations of the Superpowers. Once again the chance has been missed to press for the line of action most likely to lead in practice to non-deployment of Tomahawk, coupled with an increase of stability – namely support for rapid progress in the INF talks aimed for the 'zero option' or as near to that as is negotiable.

SHORT RANGE SYSTEMS

We turn next to those nuclear systems stationed in Western Europe which are not strategic – because they cannot reach the Soviet Union. They exist in bewildering profusion. The most important functional distinction is that of range. *Shorter range* systems are those whose coverage (400–600 miles) is effectively of Eastern Europe, excluding Russia. Apart from the Pershing I ballistic missile already mentioned, they consist entirely of aircraft, F–4, Jaguar, Buccaneer and Tornado, and F–104. *Short range* (or battle field) systems consist of Lance ballistic missiles (range seventy miles) and eight inch and 155 mm Howitzers (range 15 miles). There are also nuclear warheads for Nike Hercules high level air defence missiles, and for land mines – known as Atomic Demolition Munitions (ADMs). The next most important distinction concerns ownership and control. The Jaguar, Buccaneer and Tornado aircraft are British owned and designed to carry free-fall nuclear bombs of British manufacture which remain at all times under British control. The remaining systems are all American, capable of carrying American nuclear warheads. All but the F4 and ADMs have been sold to allies: Pershing to the Federal German Republic (FRG); F–104 and Nike to the FRG, Belgium and the Netherlands; Lance and the Howitzers to those countries and the United Kingdom. But even so, the nuclear warheads remain at all times in American ownership and custody up to the moment of discharge. The number of these systems is also great. In NATO Europe there are some 500 such aircraft, 1,000 surface to surface missiles and Howitzers, and 6,000 nuclear warheads stored at fifty different sites.[33] All these systems, apart from Pershing and ADM, have alternative non-nuclear modes of use.

It is important to recognize that we are dealing with a highly complex interlocking structure. The British components are fully integrated within the NATO system. All nuclear warheads of United States origin are subject to what is known as the Permissive Action Link (PAL). This consists of a code, and a family of devices integral or attached to the warheads and designed to reduce to a minimum the possibility of an unauthorized detonation. Only when the correct numerical code has been inserted can the weapon be fired. The code itself is a secure system which allows the using unit to obtain the proper numbers only after the PAL unlock has been authorized. The transmission of the coded signal from the controller obviously places a high premium on a prompt and accurate communication system. When the means of delivery (aircraft, missile or Howitzer) has been sold to allies, and is operated by Britain or any other European nation, the dual control implied in these arrangements is what is known as the two key system. The nuclear discharge could take place only by the most precise collaboration of the two nations concerned.

The rationale for these weapons is even more disputable than that of the longer range missiles. Ostensibly they exist to provide the necessary fire power to defeat a massive advance by forces of the Warsaw Pact. NATO doctrine specifically caters for what is ghoulishly known as nuclear 'release' if conventional forces are in danger of being overrun and there is no other way of stopping the advance. For a variety of reasons such an attack is unlikely: nevertheless it is a wholly legitimate goal of allied policy to make any such action so utterly unattractive to the Russians that even in dire emergency they would be deterred from taking it. The difficulty is that, in military terms, the use of nuclear weapons for this purpose is highly problematical.

The first reason is that nuclear 'release' is likely to be late in coming. Assume, for the sake of argument, that the Warsaw Pact did indeed launch a massive attack across the North German plain. The received wisdom suggests that it would very likely win – in the sense that it would overrun the Ruhr and the Rhine, if not the Channel ports – within days or at best a week or so: long before the full potential of NATO and in particular North America, could be brought against it. If a nuclear response is to play any part in preventing that outcome it would be needed *before* NATO forces had dissolved into disarray and Soviet forces had become inextricably co-mingled: in a matter of days or at the most a week. But, as Michael Howard has pointed out, 'the decision to authorize the use of nuclear weapons, on however limited a scale, against an adversary with

125

the Soviet Union's awesome powers of retaliation would be the most dreadful that any western statesman on either side of the Atlantic could ever be called upon to take. Politicians are not military commanders concerned primarily with victory, but the elected leaders of democracies which expect them to secure their social survival. They are not and should not be heroes. It would be at least sensible to assume that they would require time to make up their collective minds'.[34] From a military point of view this makes the timing of nuclear 'release' – even if it were desired – a highly unpredictable gamble.

Nor is there any certainty what the military effects of such use would be. There is evidence from studies that if NATO were to use nuclear weapons in such circumstances and on a limited scale, and if the Warsaw Pact replied at a similar level, though NATO might achieve some limited delay the Warsaw Pact advance could fairly soon be resumed and perhaps even more decisively than if the nuclear exchange had never taken place. An alternative view is that of Shelford Bidwell, which he says is tacitly agreed outside of paper exercises, that after an exchange of some fifty or sixty weapons the troops on either side would either bolt or go to ground in panic.[35] No-one knows.

What is almost universally agreed is that once a single nuclear weapon has been used by either side a boundary of almost unimaginable danger will have been crossed. *The Church and the Bomb* is fully justified in drawing attention to the central importance of 'escalation'. It is a metaphor drawn from the moving staircase and implies that once embarked upon the bottom step you can neither get off nor turn back, nor is there any emergency stop button. The reason is that nuclear strikes on the opposing front line are relatively ineffective. It is just here that troops are most widely dispersed and least vulnerable – either in slit trenches or under armour. Consequently the target list extends back to the second echelons; to concentration areas, bridges, air fields, marshalling yards, and control centres. And then, as Helmut Schmidt pointed out, 'who could complain if the Soviet high command, in response to destructive attacks on the Vistula Bridges involving the (albeit unintentional) widespread devastation of Warsaw proceeded simultaneously to destroy the Elbe and Rhone crossings and in so doing produce similar devastation in Hamburg, Cologne, Dusseldorf. And if we wish to lodge a complaint to what tribunal shall we take it'?[36] If this argument is accepted one should reckon, as the foreseeable consequence of such an exchange, a European death toll running once again into tens of millions, the overwhelming majority of whom would be civilian. The whole social fabric of Central Europe would be decimated – industry, hospitals, communications, trade, and government both at provincial and national level. In no possible circumstances could such an outcome be justified by reference to the defence of western values, nor yet to the triumph of Soviet socialism. In such a war there can be no winners.

Would escalation occur? Again there can be no certainty. It is a fair point that in circumstances where the Russians were deliberate aggressors, with the possession of Western Europe their desired prize, it could not conceivably be in their interest to devastate it nor could the cost ever be worthwhile. But this argument overlooks certain vital points. First the Russians have plainly said, and it is intrinsic to their doctrine, that any use by NATO of nuclear weapons in Europe will be met by massive retaliation in kind. Secondly, rather than as a deliberately planned act of annexation, war in Europe might arise much more untidily and ambiguously – perhaps as a result of recurring and worsening instability within Eastern Europe. Thirdly, if the alternative in Soviet eyes were outright defeat, in such a dire conjunction the nuclear devastation of the adversary might indeed seem the lesser of evils.

NO FIRST USE?

From these considerations three conclusions follow. First, that the only plausible function of NATO non-strategic systems is to prevent the Russians ever from using theirs by posing the threat of retaliation. So long as Russia retains such systems so must the West – but the numbers presently held are vastly in excess of what is needed for that purpose. Secondly, there would be great merit in carrying out the modest force improvement proposed by General Bernard Rogers, Supreme Allied Commander in Europe, on 28 September 1982, which he said would make it possible for NATO to mount a convincing non-nuclear defence of Western Europe.[37] According to him, the technology now exists. If the rate of annual increase of defence spending by the NATO nations were raised from the present notional 3 per cent to a genuine 4 per cent in real terms, the job could be done. But thirdly, since no such increase features in the forward planning of any European nation at present, for the time being there is probably some marginal utility in a concept of 'first use' of nuclear weapons by NATO in Europe as a means of conveying a political signal. Lord Trenchard has speculated[38] that if our conventional defences were being overwhelmed, NATO might launch a single nuclear weapon in a defined area and accompanied by clear warnings to cease aggression. Presumably the objective would be to test the possibility (as an alternative to the simple acceptance of defeat with all its consequences) that the Soviet leaders were so disconcerted at finding that they had miscalculated NATO's resolve, or so appalled at the imminent threat of precipitating the final holocaust, that they preferred to back off. While the likelihood of NATO taking any such action must be rated as exceedingly slight, and the consequences utterly unpredictable, nevertheless it need not be judged wholly irrational. The crucial point often overlooked in discussion, is that NATO has neither the means nor the will to carry out any aggression in Europe itself. The NATO leaders were transparently sincere in their declaration that 'none of our weapons will ever be used except in response to attack'.[39] The threat of aggression lies, if anywhere, upon the other side. Where nuclear weapons are concerned there is nothing to choose, on ethical grounds, between first use and retaliation. Consequently there is no merit in a 'no first use declaration' as opposed to a change in strategic substance – since this would only compound confusion, sow disarray among allies and might increase however marginally the chance of Soviet miscalculation. The essential task is to ensure not simply that nuclear weapons are never used in Europe, but that no war breaks out of any kind. In present circumstances NATO doctrine with all its inconsistencies, probably holds out the best chance of success.

Against this background the likely consequences of acting as *The Church and the Bomb* proposes can be more clearly seen. The United Kingdom would have to destroy the bombs for the Jaguar, Buccaneer and Tornado force, and no longer accept nuclear warheads under the two-key system for Lance and the Howitzers. In the integrated scene which has been described it is difficult to make any sense of this. In war, the British army component would be sandwiched initially between German and Belgian divisions with the United States formations behind them in reserve. But in action boundaries soon become blurred; artillery of one nation will be called upon to support another; and in the case of missiles targetted upon reserves in depth it is impossible to tell whom they are supporting. The air, in any case, is indivisible. While the land and air forces of all other participants on the Central Front retain their own nuclear component, to plan a non-nuclear sector of the action for the British would be militarily nonsensical. As and when it becomes possible to stage a genuinely non-nuclear defence (retaining some nuclear weapons only to deter Soviet use) then much of the present inventory could be dispensed with and it may be hoped that the short range systems (ADMs, Nike, artillery and perhaps Lance) might disappear completely. But the unilateral British rejection of these nuclear systems, in forced time, would mean the effective withdrawal of British forces from the land and air battle currently planned and conceived. The only logical way to give meaning to this would be to bring them home. It is difficult to conceive of any action more likely to destabilize the alliance. General Rogers has recently explained that the forces now available to him are only marginally adequate for initial defence. A reduction (let alone withdrawal) of British land and air forces would have a 'fundamental and critical effect on our long established strategy and overall deterrent and defensive posture'.[40] He has in mind not least the psychological impact upon other members of the alliance. It is in fact very doubtful, bearing in mind current political misgivings in Belgium, Holland, and not least the United States, whether the alliance in anything like its present form would survive.

It remains to discuss two maritime ingredients in the British nuclear involvement, and this can be done very simply. The two Sea Harrier squadrons operating from anti-submarine carriers can deliver British free-fall nuclear bombs; various maritime helicopters ashore and afloat (notably Sea King) can deliver British nuclear depth bombs; and the four Nimrod maritime patrol squadrons based in the United Kingdom can be equipped with United States nuclear depth bombs – presumably under some form of two-key control.[41] Since the British navy bears the brunt of keeping the Atlantic sea lanes open in war for the United States supply and reinforcement, the task is of comparable importance to the land/air defence of Western Europe in terms of Atlantic cohesion. An ordinance of nuclear self denial on the part of the British would make arrant nonsense in alliance terms – the more so since a nuclear depth bomb is a totally defensive weapon, almost wholly devoid of collateral effects upon non-combatants, and not inherently escalatory.

There remains the provision by the United Kingdom of facilities for a submarine depot ship and floating dock, in Holy Loch, for the United States nuclear ballistic missile submarine fleet. This is an arrangement which antedated the Polaris agreement at Nassau though it played some part in those negotiations.[42] But even if the British Polaris fleet were to be pensioned off prematurely there would be no case for seeking to abrogate the Holy Loch agreement. Whereas the United States Government – as has been suggested earlier in this chapter – might stomach the former with good grace they could scarcely fail to take the latter amiss. The US Polaris submarines operating out of Holy Loch are not under NATO control, and the British Government has no say in their employment, but there is an understanding that the deployment and use of the depot ship in periods of emergency would be a matter of joint consultation between the two governments.[43] Plainly these facilities form an important means of deploying the US nuclear deterrent effectively. Abrogation of the agreement could only be seen as a direct political affront on the part of America's original and closest nuclear ally. As a means of cementing alliance solidarity and influencing the United States in disarmament negotiations it would be singularly inappropriate.

INTERNATIONAL COMPARISONS

Having thus considered piecemeal the various elements in British nuclear provision and involvement it remains to review the scene at large to see whether the whole may not be larger than the parts. Britain, after all, has played a part in the origins of nuclear weapons technology and is implicated with these weapons both nationally and in the alliance context in more different ways than any other European nation. Is it not possible that the renunciation on our part would have some special value as an example to other nations, either as a stop to proliferation, or as an encouragement to the superpowers to make better progress in their own arms control negotiations? Reflection suggests the reverse. *The Church and the Bomb* is most misleading in its discussion of international comparisons.[44] The FRG and Italy are described as 'non- nuclear weapons states' – which is true in terms of the ownership of warheads but totally untrue of their possession of substantial numbers of nuclear delivery means (aircraft, missiles, guns) and acceptance of the United States nuclear warheads under the two-key control. Norway and Denmark are said to refuse bases for US nuclear weapons on their soil in peace time – which is quite true, for good alliance reasons. But these countries do not object in principle to NATO's defensive concept; they accepted the plan for deployment of Pershing and Cruise, including their share of infrastructure costs; and the presence of United States nuclear-armed forces on their territory is certainly not ruled out in war.

The Republic of Ireland is described as 'militarily neutral but politically committed'. In fact the Republic has made no commitment. The only analogue to a Britain which remained a signatory of the North Atlantic Treaty but totally rejected nuclear involvement of any kind would be Iceland – which has no armed forces anyway. The report says that such a stance need not be hypocritical and that can be conceded. The point is that there is no merit in it either. The aim, it will be recalled, is 'marginally' to reduce the nuclear weaponry of NATO. In other words, Britain, while rejecting for her part the whole basis upon which deterrence is sought, so freeing herself from presumed moral odium, will seek to continue enjoying the fruits of that deterrence in peace and freedom. As Sir Clive Rose has pointed out it is asking us to swallow too much.[45] And since this is to be imposed upon our allies without negotiations – save over timing – it is also asking them to swallow too much. 'It is quite unrealistic to believe that it could be foisted on our allies, all of whom currently take the view that unilateral policy would seriously damage any prospect for multilateral negotiations'.

Nor is there anything surprising in this conclusion. The truth is that the authors of *The Church and the Bomb* seek nuclear disarmament for its own sake, in pursuit of what they believe to be the Christian decision. Dodging the logic they seek to apply this precept to Britain, and Britain alone, because to do so more widely would be – as they accurately perceive – highly dangerous. The concept of making renunciation 'a unilateral step within a multilateral process' is dragged in as an afterthought. If one were to begin with this objective then the point would be quite obvious that the best way to promote multilateral negotiations is precisely to take part in them – in as hard headed a way as is possible – and with the aim of securing as rapid and far-reaching results as possible within the realms of prudence. This in itself will require reduction in Britain's nuclear stance – probably the abrogation of complete capabilities – but always in concert with allies as to principle as well as to timing and to consequentials.

Here is a cause for the Christian Churches, in all the countries, to pursue with honesty, clear sightedness, logic and the pragmatism which is the report's strongest point.

That then becomes a duty.

Notes

1. J. A. Baker (ed) *The Church and the Bomb*, London: Hodder & Stoughton, 1982, p. 154.
2. Paul Oestreicher in a letter to *The Times*, 22 November 1982.
3. J.A. Baker, op. cit. p. 134.
4. ibid. p. 159.
5. ibid. p. 134.
6. ibid. p. 139.
7. P. Oestreicher, loc. cit.
8. J.A. Baker, op. cit. pp. 40.
9. P. Oestreicher, loc. cit.
10. op. cit. p. 160.
11. According to Mr Peter Blaker in the House of Commons, 27 July 1981.
12. *Defence Open Government Documents* (DOGD) 80/23 and 82/1. (11 March 1982)
13. *Statement on the Defence Estimates 1981: Cmnd. 8212–1 para. 208.*
14. *The French, though signatories of the North Atlantic Treaty, are not formally part of NATO. Nevertheless, it is recognized that, in practice, the French strategic capability represented a second centre of decision in Europe.*
15. *DOGD 80/23, pp. 3, 4.*
16. *Quoted in D. Nunnerley, President Kennedy and Britain*, London: Bodley Head, 1972, p. 77.

17. The Report would, of course, prefer to see the money reinvested in quite different ways (p. 157), but once again recognize that this might not be possible (p. 139).

18. *Statement on the Defence Estimates* 1982: Cmnd. 8529–1 para. 102.

19. *Arms Control and Disarmament Agreements*, US Arms Control and Disarmament Agency, 1982, edn. p. 86.

20. N. A. Simms, 'Britain, Chemical Weapons and Disarmament', Armament and Disarmament Information Unit of Sussex University (ADIU). Report No. 2., vol. 3, July/August 1980.

21. Reported in the *Daily Telegraph*, 22 December 1982.

22. J.A. Baker, op. cit. p. 139.

23. *The Military Balance* 1982–3, London: International Institute of Strategic Studies, p. 137.

24. Statement on Defence Estimates, 1981. Cmnd. 8212–1, paras 217–220.

25. *The Military Balance*, 1982–3, p. 112.

26. *Daily Telegraph* 22 December 1982. This reports that 275 SS–4 and 16 SS–5 are still operationally sited.

27. SS–4 and SS–5 have enormous warheads (1MT) but are relatively inaccurate. From some points of view the much more discriminate SS–20 presents a less horrendous threat.

28. Donald R. Cotter 'NATO Theatre Forces', *Strategic Review*, vol. ix., no. 2., (Spring 1982).

29. *The Military Balance* 1982–3, op. cit. p. 137.

30. Statement on Defence Estimates 1981, para 216. At the same time the US Government undertook to withdraw 1,000 nuclear warheads unilaterally, and to withdraw further warheads on a one for one basis as the new missiles were installed.

31. Simon Lunn, 'Cruise Missiles and the prospects for Arms Control', *ADIU Report*, Vol. 3., no. 5., September/October 1981.

32. It is no let out to say that *The Church and the Bomb* (pp. 160, 140) proposes negotiations with Britain's allies since it is made clear that such consultation would concern only timing and consequentials, not the principles – and that the time for decision is short.

33. Gregory Treverton 'Nuclear Weapons in Europe' *Adelphi Paper* no. 168, London: IISS, 1981, p. 13.

34. 'NATO and the year of Europe', *Round Table*, October 1973.

35. I cannot trace this reference. A more measured rendering of the same theme is in the same author's *Modern Warfare*, London, Alan Lane 1973, p. 191.

36. *Defence or Retaliation*, Oliver Boyd, 1962, p. 99.

37. *The Economist*, 2 October 1982, p. 140.

38. House of Lords, *Motion on the Humble Address*, October 1982, Column 105.

39. *Arms Control and Disarmament*, no. 13, August 1982, (FCO Pamphlet) p. 11.

40. *The Times* ,13 December 1982.
41. *Statement on the Defence Estimates* 1981 (Cmnd 6 8212–1, para 223). Torpedoes can of course be fitted with nuclear warheads but the UK does not appear to possess any.
42. Kevin Harrison 'From Independence to Dependence, Blue Streak, Skybolt, Nassau and Polaris', *RUSI Journal*, December 1982, p. 27.
43. Fred Mulley, *Politics of Western Defence*, Thames & Hudson, 1982, p. 27.
44. J.A. Baker, op. cit., pp. 134–40.
45. Letter to *The Times*, 10 November 1982.

APPENDIX

The Meaning of Deterrence
by Michael Quinlan

Michael Quinlan, a Roman Catholic, is a civil servant. Until recently he had spent most of his career in the defence field, with considerable involvement in British and NATO nuclear deterrence planning, especially between 1977 and 1981 when under both Labour and Conservative Governments he was Deputy Under-Secretary of State (Policy and Programmes) at the Ministry of Defence. We re-print below two talks, the first given on 2 July 1981 to a Civil Defence Conference at York, the second on 24 March 1982 in a Lenten lecture series organized by the Dunamis Group at St James's Piccadilly. The substance of these talks was previously published in *The Tablet* and *Crucible* respectively.

Preventing War
(Talk: 2.7.81)

I am due to talk to you this morning about the concept of deterrence, the concept around which the Governments of both parties for whom I have worked as a civil servant in this field have built British defence policy for the past thirty years. Now that concept itself is a pretty old one – in one form or another it goes back to the Romans, and beyond. But it is only since 1945 that the word 'deterrence' has become so familiar a part of our standard vocabulary; and none of us at this conference needs any long reminder of why that is so. On two days in August 1945 there was proof, in the most direct way possible, that the ability to destroy in war, which had been progressively growing throughout the history of at least recent centuries, had suddenly made an abrupt and terrible leap upwards.

And what that leap meant, as was very quickly realized, was that war to the maximum of mankind's power could never again be viewed, as it might have been in the past, as just an inferior and unpleasant way of managing international affairs; it ceased to be a way of managing international affairs at all. The idea of preventing war – at least all-out war between top-level powers – acquired an immediate and absolute cogency, a compulsion, which it had never had before. And in turn, because Governments have been able to find no surer practical method of prevention than deterrence, deterrence has become the centrepiece of security policy.

CENTRAL AIM

So deterrence today is above all about the prevention of nuclear war. But that is not all that it is about; the omission of the limiting word 'nuclear' in front of 'war' in the title of my talk is not accidental. It does seem to me very important to recognize that the ghastly events of August 1945 did not mean that war suddenly became nasty having previously been nice. It had not previously been nice. I myself have never had to fight. But I do remember the London Blitz (a mild affair, of course, by later standards), and I have walked some of the battlefields of World War I – I've looked up at the 54,000 names carved on just one memorial at the Menin Gate, and looked out across those silent acres upon acres of neat white crosses in the cemeteries of Passchendaele and the Somme. World War II took the lives, in one way or another, of something like fifty million people before most of us had ever heard of a place called Hiroshima. We are, I suspect, sometimes lulled by the jargon we use – we talk of non-nuclear weapons as being 'conventional', with a flavour of acceptability, almost of cosiness. But non-nuclear war was appalling in World War II, and the weapons available for it are far more powerful now than they were then – not least the chemical weapons available at superpower level.

So I believe that it is imperative to prevent all war, not just nuclear war. And this is given added force, in my view, by a further factor. Non-nuclear war is not just appalling in itself; it is also the likeliest route to nuclear war. The notion of nuclear war coming out of the blue is far-fetched; scenarios of the holocaust being launched just because some computer goes on the blink are plain rubbish. The risk of nuclear war would be most real in a situation where bitter conflict had already broken out at a lower level; so we have an added reason for making sure that it does not break out at all.

The object therefore has to be prevention of all war, not just nuclear war, between the two great power blocs. Does the requirement for a policy of deterrence follow immediately from that? Well, no it doesn't – not quite.

Another way of avoiding nuclear war would be to decide consciously on a policy of non-resistance – a policy, that is, of surrender if necessary. But the Governments of the West have consistently taken a different view. They have judged, firstly, that they could not rule out the possibility that our way of life, our freedom, might be threatened by external force; and secondly that our way of life, for all its imperfections, was so much preferable to the main alternative as to be worth a great deal of effort to preserve. Now you can find people, in good faith, who will contest one or other or both those propositions. I'm not going to argue them here; I note simply that Governments of both parties in office in Britain have essentially accepted them as the premises of their security policy. And when you accept those propositions and set them alongside our earlier aim – we must avoid war, yet there may be a threat, and surrender to it would not be tolerable – then you are led, inexorably, to a policy of deterrence. Put another way, deterrence, it seems to me, is the policy you have to have if you believe in the possibility of grave threat and yet want to continue in both peace and freedom – neither red nor dead. I might note in passing that under the main alternative political system, in its various forms from Lenin and Stalin to Pol Pot, many millions of people were not given even that choice. But our aim is never to have to face it at all; and deterrence is a key element of the policies on which our Governments have consistently relied for ensuring that. It does not, of course, assume a constant and implacable hostile desire to attack us; it simply judges, in the light perhaps of history, that we cannot prudently assume that we never would be attacked even if attack on us were a soft option.

HOW DETERRENCE WORKS

Let me now turn to what deterrence means, and how it works, in the world as it exists now. In essence, deterrence means transmitting a basically simple message. It says, to whom it may concern, that if you attack me, I will resist; I will go on resisting until you stop or until my strength fails; and, if it is the latter, my strength will not fail before I have inflicted on you

139

damage so heavy that you will be much worse off at the end than if you had never started; so do not start. We seek, essentially, to get that message across.

So far, you may well think, I have led you by a rather slow road to a routine conclusion. Well, maybe so; but from now on things get more complicated. Communicating that simple-sounding message in the real world is a complex affair, and it needs hard and clear thinking – even uncomfortable thinking. In one sense, that thinking is more difficult because we have little fact and experience to go on. The data on nuclear war are scanty, thank God; just two isolated uses, half a lifetime ago, by someone who had these weapons against someone who hadn't. Beyond that we are working in theory and inference and hypothesis. That's not to say we're dealing in hot air and guesswork. It would be very dangerous to suppose that, for the penalties for being careless about thinking things through might one day be appalling; we can't afford to polish our deterrence theory by experiment, by trial and error; one failure will be one too many. So however convoluted or abstract, or even repugnant, we may find the outpourings of the strategic theorists, it is not a mark of wisdom to brush them all impatiently aside. The penalty for over-elaboration and over-insurance may perhaps be some waste of time and money; but the penalty for skimping our thinking, and for under-insurance, may be almost infinite.

Thinking deterrence through is quite a tough intellectual discipline, and scholars have filled libraries with books about it. We have to reflect on hypothetical sequences of events, thinking many moves ahead, so that no sequence could leave a potential adversary with a window, a risk-free track. We have to consider not just how our own leaders would feel able to act (though that obviously matters) but also how an adversary would react from a background of very different attitudes and standards, and not just now but in future circumstances which may be very different – perhaps much more awkward, for us or for him, than today's. We need deterrence that will work not only in easy circumstances, in calm, but also under pressure. We have to work in abstract concepts and metaphors – thresholds and escalation ladders and signalling and so on – which can mislead us if we get careless about their meaning, if we mistake them for the reality which they are shorthand for.

All that said, I do not propose to attempt to lead you now through all the intricacies of NATO's deterrence theory. I want just to pick out a few themes which, in my view, current debate on these issues – debate whose renewed vigour, I may say, I personally welcome – tends to misunderstand.

My first point is about the relationship between nuclear and conventional forces in deterrence. One can legitimately argue about what the right proportions are between the two, either for individual countries or collectively. But people sometimes talk as though they were alternative methods of deterrence. They are not. NATO's deterrence, in today's world, needs them both, and neither can work without the other. No amount of nuclear power will be credible if we have no effective lesser response available to minor attacks; and no amount of conventional power can be sure of keeping us safe if there is one-sided nuclear power ranged against us. It is worth noting, incidentally, that conventional forces come far more expensive than nuclear ones, so that people who want both more reliance on conventional forces and also lower defence expenditure are riding horses in somewhat divergent directions. Indeed, the vast bulk of military expenditure worldwide goes on conventional forces; if there is an arms race that needs to be stopped or slowed in order to release resources for, say, the Third World, that race is sharpest and costliest in the conventional field, not the nuclear. But that is by the way. My main point is that East/West deterrence cannot operate in separate nuclear and conventional boxes, or with either of them alone; and the reason is that East/West war itself cannot be guaranteed to operate in separate boxes, especially when we face a potential adversary with the particular strengths of the Warsaw Pact. However we may decide to share out particular tasks within NATO Alliance, the Alliance as a whole has to have both kinds of forces, interacting and interdependent in deterrence; and we all, I suggest, have to accept a collective burden of responsibility for that.

'WARFIGHTING'

I should like to come next to the concept of 'warfighting', because confusion about this seems to me to be at present the single most prevalent misconception about deterrence. The argument runs, very briefly, that Western thinking about nuclear war is in the course of making a most dangerous shift – that with the introduction of weapons that are for example more accurate or of more limited effect, and with more conscious and systematic planning for nuclear contingencies short of instant all-out holocaust, we are moving away from the concept of deterrence and beginning to plan for really fighting nuclear wars.

Now I do not want to seem harsh about a worry which I know is often sincerely felt; but it really is a total fallacy, resting on a complete misconception. The fact is that the deterrent effect of weapons and plans is not something separate from and independent of their capability for actual use; it operates precisely *through* capability for actual use. If weapons are not capable of realistic use they cannot deter; the more difficult they are to use in any rational way the less credible they are, and accordingly the less likely to deter; and if an adversary thinks we have no meaningful plans for use he will think we have no serious will to resist. Like it or not, there lies inescapably at the heart of deterrence a kind of paradox. The more likely it is that you will use your capability if you need to, the less likely it is that you will ever be faced with the need. And the converse is equally true. So people who recoil from more accurate weapons and less widespread targeting plans – I wonder, in passing, whether they advocate more destructive and less accurate weapons and more widespread targeting plans? – are in fact proposing less credible deterrence and therefore more risk of war.

Let it be clear, though, that what I am saying is that we must have weapons capable of credible use, and plans to match. I am not saying that that use should be, or that it even can be, for winning victories in the classical sense. I simply do not believe in such a notion; nor does NATO; nor did the US Secretary of Defense when he explained the up-dated American planning concepts which aroused so much comment in 1980. At least in the West, Governments clearly accept that ideas of actually winning wars with nuclear weapons have no reality. When both sides possess in effect almost infinite destructive power the idea of wearing down the other side's power to the point of exhaustion, like Hitler's in 1945, becomes simply obsolete. Indeed, the only thing our nuclear weapons can really do for us – but it is a vital thing – is to place that basic truth plainly before the eyes of anyone contemplating aggression against us. But they cannot make that truth plain – they cannot even keep it true – if they do not exist, or if they are not capable of use in ways which an aggressor could find believable. Deterrence and a capability for warfighting – not warwinning, but warfighting; that is, meaningful resistance – are not alternatives or rivals; they are two sides of a single coin.

ESCALATION

I turn now, briefly, to the matter of escalation. I said a moment ago that NATO does not believe that nuclear wars can be won in anything like the traditional sense. Still less, accordingly, does NATO believe in the idea of winning limited nuclear wars, in the sense of using nuclear weapons to help in the conduct of classical military operations to a successful and decisive conclusion. There are two main sorts of reason why this cannot be a sensible concept to rely upon. Firstly, the destruction in even a so-called limited war, for example across the territory of Western Europe, could be appalling. But secondly and even more fundamentally, the size of East/West nuclear armouries and the means available to deliver them are such that whatever the course of any limited engagement with nuclear weapons, the side temporarily coming off worst would always have a powerful alternative to defeat – the alternative of raising the stakes, of escalation.

Now we need, in my view, to think particularly carefully about what lessons that has for our policies and our plans. You will find people who say that it proves that the possession of tactical or theatre nuclear weapons is pointless; or that escalation is a certainty. It does not in fact prove either of those things – rather the contrary. Escalation is not an inexorable scientific process; it is a matter of human decision, to be taken moreover in circumstances of which we have fortunately no fully comparable past experience. We do not know, and I hope we never find out, precisely how statesmen – or soldiers, for that matter – will react if these fearful weapons ever start to fly about. Anyone, however, eminent, who tells us that escalation is a certainty, or who purports to put a tidy figure of percentage probability upon it, is talking through his hat. The reality is surely this. No aggressor could afford to bring down thousands

143

of nuclear weapons on his homeland. If he attacks, therefore, it must have been on a calculation that the defender would lack the resolve to use the weapons. There must be at least some possibility that when met by a nuclear response, even on a comparatively modest scale, he may re-assess his earlier calculation, and prefer to back off rather than take the risks of going on. NATO's policy in the field of theatre nuclear weapons is based on maximizing that possibility, be it large or small. It is entirely sensible – indeed necessary – to do that, while at the same time continuing to recognize that whatever we do it will remain no more than a possibility; and that because it is precarious and the risks appalling (risks, of course, which bear on the calculations of both sides, not on those of the defender alone) the central aim must remain outright prevention – that is, preventing the whole process of East/West war from ever starting.

What that argument amounts to, expressed another way round, is that we must aim at outright prevention, but that we must also do whatever we can, imperfect though it is bound to be, to leave ourselves courses of practical action available if outright prevention fails. That is plain common sense; but it has a double value in the deterrent context. The more evident it is to an aggressor that we have courses of continuing resistance available if war comes, the less likely it is that he will reckon war – with all its dangers for him too – to be worth his while at all; so outright prevention is itself reinforced. And that, in my judgement, applies to the whole business of preparedness, which is of course of especial interest to this conference.

I need not tell any of you that there is a line of argument heard nowadays from time to time, that civil defence precautions ought not to be taken. The argument has perhaps three strands. First, that civil defence is a cruel deception, because tens of millions will die anyway if there is an all-out nuclear war. I shall not spend long on that. None of you, and certainly not I, ever imagine that the effects of nuclear war could be less than ghastly; but the argument implies, in logic, that if the effects of a disaster cannot be reduced to zero, preparations which could in some degree keep down their scale are a cruel deception. It says, if you like, that we should not wear seatbelts because they will not abolish all road casualties. The second strand of the argument is that civil defence preparation means we are expecting a nuclear war. That seems to me to say that people who wear seat-belts are expecting to have more crashes than people who do not. And the third strand is that civil defence preparation means that one is actually disposed towards nuclear war. It is worth asking, if that were logical, what inference we should draw from the enormous Russian effort in civil defence, and what lesson might then follow for our own defence policies. But of course the argument isn't logical; it says, in effect, that people who wear seat-belts tend to be more dangerous drivers than people who do not, which is observably untrue. The fact is, for deterrence, that if you take no precautions at all you transmit to an adversary the message that you are simply not prepared to think about the consequences if he does attack and you then resist; and that message does not underpin deterrence – it undermines it. There is here another of those hard paradoxes. To say that you are not prepared to contemplate the failure of deterrence is actually to make that failure more likely.

Let me make it clear that I am not suggesting that in order to support civil defence it is necessary to believe in the standard NATO view of deterrence. That is plainly not so. The case for civil defence is one, I venture to think, which is valid also for those who take other views, including the outright pacifist view. But I do say that civil defence effort is perfectly compatible with, and indeed helpful to, support for and confidence in deterrence.

STABILITY OF DETERRENCE

Mention of confidence in deterrence carries me to the final main point I wanted to talk about – the stability of deterrence. A lot of people, including some of great distinction, talk as though the whole system of deterrence was desperately precarious, and perhaps becoming increasingly so. With all respect to those who deserve it, I believe this is mistaken. We must not be complacent, of course; the price of stability is, I do not doubt, continuing vigilance. And technical competition in many areas goes on unremittingly, save for a few where arms control agreements (of which I wish there were more) have slowed it or sealed it off – the precise military balance is not static. But that does not mean that the overall system is unstable. There are many reasons to the contrary. There is, for example, the very size of the armouries and the knowledge of what they can do. No-one who lives with the facts and has to think about them can ever be trigger-happy, or other than enormously cautious. I venture to speak as someone who has worked with these matters on and off for over twenty years, and who has not, I hope, grown insensitive to the realities – I keep pictures of Hiroshima and Nagasaki in view from my office desk as a stark reminder. Five-figure numbers of these awful weapons on each side are far too many, and I wish the Russians had accepted the Carter proposals for deep cuts; but at least these vast numbers do mean that no-one can suppose that he could somehow ride the punch on tolerable terms. Next, despite ups and downs, communication, understanding and agreement between the two sides is far more extensive than it was, say, in the 1960s. The SALT I and SALT II agreements are in practice being kept, even though the first has theoretically expired and the second has not been ratified. There is a Standing Consultative Commission meeting regularly to monitor the agreements reached. Anti-ballistic-missile deployments, which in the 1960s looked a real threat to stability, are now closely constrained by treaty. There are hotlines, regularly exercised. There are practical agreements to avoid conflict incidents, to explain accidents, to notify in advance missile launch tests whose purpose might be misunderstood, to consult together about dangerous international situations. Intelligence, especially through satellite photography, means that each side knows far more surely than before what the other is doing. The delivery systems themselves are far less vulnerable to pre-emptive strike than they used to be, so there is far less incentive to launch first and ask questions afterwards. Mobile cruise missiles will be much less vulnerable on the ground than the present F111s and Vulcans; and it is perhaps worth remembering that in the mid-60s Britain's own strategic force relied on V-bombers held on runway alert and needing to get off the ground within two or three minutes, whereas our force now rests on submarines hidden at sea. And at the political level I believe that even the passing years themselves, and the successive crises surmounted, deepen the inbuilt habit and understanding, on both sides, that nuclear weapons must not be used, and that whatever the disagreements the two great power blocs therefore simply must not come to blows. I do not claim certainty here; certainty is not to be had. But I do believe that claims of perilous instability, of a world teetering on the brink, are neither well-founded nor helpful to peace.

It is time for me to conclude. I do not like the system of deterrence centred on nuclear weapons; it is an unlikeable thing, even an ugly one. I wish we had a better system, and I hope discussion and challenge in the search for a better system will continue. Meanwhile, I hope we can continue to improve the present system, making it still safer and if possible less expensive. It cannot solve everything – it is not a recipe for universal peace; it does not claim to prevent the Third World conflicts in which 'conventional' wars have killed something like ten million people over the last thirty-five years (while nuclear wars haven't happened at all). But within its context – the context of NATO and the Warsaw Pact – our deterrence has worked; it still works; I believe it can go on working, and working safely, *provided* we stay clearheaded in identifying what it requires and resolute in doing what it requires. Deterrence is, in essence, a system for helping to cope with a hard world in which we have to reconcile two realities – that the sources of deep conflict exist; and that alongside those sources there also exist the means of conducting conflict in intolerably destructive ways. I see no safer system than this now within our reach; and until I do, I would not choose to gamble by discarding this one.

Nuclear Weapons: A View of the Moral Problem
(*Talk: 24.3.82*)

I am a Civil Servant by trade, and I have spent most of my career dealing with defence, though I am at present serving in the Treasury. In my defence days I had a lot to do with nuclear policy; and I imagine that is why I have been asked to talk today. I am however in no sense here as a government spokesman. I do not intend to go into specific political or technical questions like Trident or Cruise missiles; indeed, officials cannot be free, even when speaking in a personal capacity as I do now, to express opinions about these in public. I intend to address a more fundamental question, a moral question. People who know that I am a Christian – I am a Roman Catholic – have sometimes asked me how it is that, professing to be a follower of Christ, I could bear to have anything whatever to do

147

with destructive instruments as appalling as nuclear weapons. That is a hard question; let me explain how I approach it.

If we are to think straight about any ethical issue in this field, whether general or detailed, I believe we must first grasp the nature of the basic problem. That problem comes from the existence side by side of two bitter facts, and from the task that falls upon our generation of being virtually the first that has to live with them both.

Fact number one is a relatively new fact, about the technology of war. Weapons have been growing steadily more destructive for most of the past two centuries, and by World War II they had already become terrible. But in 1945 there was a sudden and ghastly leap, made plain at Hiroshima and Nagasaki. Since then we have had to live, as mankind will for the rest of history, with the clear meaning of that leap – that there is irrevocably available to our knowledge not just more force than before, but virtually boundless force, transforming the whole significance of any war between major world powers or groups.

That is fact number one. Fact number two is an older fact, about human nature – about ourselves. This is that the motives and failings and pressures that in the past have brought men to war are still there – they have not conveniently gone away because of the new fact number one, however much we might wish they had. The world has contained in the past – and the very recent past – evil leaders and evil state systems, capable of savage aggression and oppression against others on a huge scale. Christian charity does not mean being sentimental or soft-headed about realities like these. Whether the world contains such forces now may be a matter of opinion; but no-one can sensibly assert that it could never in the future contain them again.

Given all that, the problem for the Christian is to decide what practical principles are to guide his actions in this difficult world where there exist side by side both the possibility of deep conflict with aggression and the means of conducting conflict in horrifying ways.

In the long run, of course, the positive Christian aim must be to dissolve the problem; and I shall come back to that later. But I believe we have to recognise that for the present we cannot just wish the problem away. To pretend that because it ideally ought not to exist it therefore does not exist is escapism, not Christianity. We have to face it, and to choose a way of coping with it.

Now there are ultimately two alternative ways of coping. One is deterrence; the other is renunciation. I should like to say something about each. But I want initially to say four things about the approach to the choice itself.

HARD CHOICES

The first thing is that the choice is extremely hard, intellectually, morally and practically; and the beginning of wisdom and of honesty is simply to recognise that. Each of the alternatives has to face very grave difficulties, including ethical difficulties; these do not weigh upon one side alone.

The second thing is that in this hard choice both sides of the Western debate want peace and freedom. Both perhaps have their wilder fringes, but the mainstreams share these goals. The central argument is not between people who hate the idea of nuclear war and people who don't, any more than it is between people who are soft on totalitarian tyranny and people who aren't. In my view, the sort of polemic – wherever it comes from in the political spectrum – which presents the debate in those terms merely obscures and trivialises it.

My third point is that I believe we must be prepared to see the ethical question from the standpoint of the West, the free world, as a whole, of which we are a committed and crucial member. I would see, for example, no moral merit in a position which washed Britain's hands of nuclear affairs on basic ethical grounds, but which then continued, explicitly or implicitly, to rely for its security on American nuclear strength continuing to counterbalance the Soviet Union.

And my fourth point is that Christian debate must seek to arrive at principles and guidelines which will be valid for very hard cases, not just for easier ones; and for the long-term future, not just for the next few years. Let me expand on that. There are those who think that the Soviet Union is essentially and reliably peaceful, and those who think it might sooner or later behave aggressively if Western weakness were to make that a far safer option than it is now. Again, there are those who think the system of deterrence is highly precarious, and those who think it is extremely stable. Either way, these are matters for political or technical judgement, not for moral judgement; and Christian ethical principles must cater for different combinations of views, honestly held, on these practical issues . It will not do, I suggest, to claim absolute validity for principles which Christians could prudently and responsibly follow only on (say) very left-wing views of the world, or only on very right-wing views. To put the same basic point a different way, we must be prepared to test our principles against awkward hypotheses. We must be prepared to answer to ourselves honestly, for example, whether the moral imperatives we recommend, whether pointing to deterrence or to unconditional renunciation, would still have been valid and compelling in face of a nuclear-armed Hitler. It is not a Christian attitude to challenge God by assuming that he will never allow such a person to exist, any more than Christians of the time could assume that he would not allow an Attila or a Genghis Khan, or Hitler himself.

BASIC ALTERNATIVES

Let me now say a little about each of the main alternatives – their strengths and their weaknesses.

I take first the path of renunciation, the path of unilateral – that is, one-sided – disarmament taken all the way. (I say 'taken all the way' because it is perfectly possible to undertake limited measures of one-sided nuclear disarmament even within the deterrence context, and there are plenty of examples on the Western side, like the unrequited American withdrawal of a thousand nuclear warheads from Europe a year or so ago.) But the true path of renunciation as a moral imperative I take to be total and unconditional.

Now this must be powerfully attractive to Christians. It would mean that the West could never engage in nuclear exchange, never endanger or kill anyone with nuclear weapons. Taken in isolation, that must be good; and I respect those who choose that path. But my respect, to be frank, is limited unless they at the same time face up honestly and clearly to the likely consequences; after all, likely consequences are part of what determines the moral quality of any act. And the consequences for the West may be that we would leave ourselves effectively defenceless against any determined aggressor who possesses nuclear weapons.

150

There is a school of thought which sees some prospect of security in methods of defence which do not in any way entail the possession of nuclear weapons. This school deserves to be listened to seriously. But it is a minority opinion which has as yet nowhere near proved its case, and I think most people do not find it very plausible. Its critics suggest that what seems to work for Sweden or Switzerland today could not be relied upon to work for others whose circumstances and responsibilities are very different, especially in the transformed global situation which complete one-sided Western nuclear disarmament would create. The critics also point out, more fundamentally, that the whole trouble with nuclear weapons is that they provide overwhelming force, and that it cannot be very likely that systems opposing them with far less force would really work if the aggressor were determined enough; after all, one of the key and successful aims of the American use of atomic weapons in 1945 was precisely to prevent a long-drawn-out defence of the Japanese homeland by conventional forces.

Now obviously there is room for discussion about all this. But to put matters at their mildest, it is at least possible to believe in good faith (and I think most commentators would so believe) that against a determined nuclear adversary non-nuclear defence could not in the end succeed; and Christian ethical principles must cater for the possibility that this belief is right. If it is right, then the consequence of one-sided and unconditional nuclear renunciation is to leave us effectively defenceless against such a nuclear adversary. Renunciation then amounts to saying, in effect, that the right Christian response to the discovery of boundless military force is simply to leave the aggressive and the unscrupulous to wield it unopposed for any purposes they like, even if those turn out to be the purposes of Hitler or Stalin or Pol Pot. Frankly, I have difficulty in agreeing that that must be what Christ Our Lord requires us to accept, not only for ourselves individually but for our neighbours and our children for the rest of time.

That seems to me the fundamental difficulty about the path of renunciation. But I recognized earlier that both paths were beset with grave difficulty; so let me turn to the difficulty of the alternative path, the path of preventing aggression by deterrence. This seems to me to have potentially two aspects.

The first concerns practical consequences, and I have touched on it already. It is the question whether deterrence is a very precarious system, or a very stable one, or something in between. I myself believe, and if there were time would be prepared to argue at length, that it is very stable, precisely because the consequences of its breakdown could plainly be so appalling. Those who hold contrary opinions on this are entitled to arrive at very different views from mine about the value of deterrence. But that is a matter of practical judgement; it is not in itself a matter of Christian ethics, either way, though it clearly has ethical implications.

The other potential aspect of difficulty for deterrence is much more directly ethical in character; it is about whether it can be moral, even where the aim is to prevent war and even where the likelihood of success in that aim is very high, to contemplate and indeed prepare for the hypothesis of actually using nuclear weapons if aggression ever pushes us that far. For me, as for many others who also on balance prefer the path of deterrence, that is the most complex and most difficult ethical issue in the whole of this subject, and Christian thinking on it is diverse and unsettled. To attempt to go into it fully in a few minutes now would merely guarantee a half-baked presentation, so I shall not pretend to offer a thorough analysis, still less one to which everyone on the pro-deterrence side would necessarily subscribe. Let me simply say that I do believe it possible to find a legitimate moral basis for possessing nuclear weapons provided that the aim is truly deterrence of aggression, and provided that the likelihood of success in that aim is high.

In my opinion, our deterrent planning cannot be bluff; we could not operate, morally or practically, on the basis of some secret determination that we would never in fact use the weapons even in the face of nuclear attack. At the same time, our planning need not and must not be genocidal; effective deterrence does not inescapably imply pure counter-population targetting – though it has to recognise that any plans adequate to deter would, if ever implemented, cause awesome destruction and death. It is nevertheless conceivable that in extreme circumstances that might be a less terrible outcome than to concede world conquest to another Hitler or Stalin. And if planning accordingly makes it immensely improbable – as I believe it does – that we will ever have to face that fearful comparison and choice in real life, then I regard such planning as legitimate when matched against the alternative; the alternative, so far as I can see, not merely of risking hostile domination but also of making war actually more likely, not less.

For what the existence of nuclear weapons on both sides has done is to make it clear to even the most reckless statesman that starting war between East and West is not remotely a rational option. Any war, that is not just nuclear war; and I thank God for that, since even what we nowadays cosily call 'conventional' war would in modern East/West circumstances be an evil of colossal dimensions. But what prevents war from being a rational option is above all the presence of appalling power on both sides; take it away from one side alone, and then for the other side war may again seem a highly rational option, just as it was at the nuclear level for the United States in 1945.

POSITIVE GOALS

But let me come back now to what I believe must be for Christians the positive angle to all this. I began by stating the basic problem, of near-boundless force available in a world where aggressively evil state systems can exist. In my view a policy of renunciation would amount to an attempt to deal with the problem by acting as though it isn't really there; while deterrence faces the problem and tries to manage it. But neither of them of course actually solves it – they are simply rival ways of trying to live with it. The major task for Christians must surely be to pray and to work, so far as we can, gradually to dissolve the problem – to create between East and West the kind of international understanding and openness that exists between Britain and the United States, or more strikingly now between France and West Germany, where states simply do not have to take seriously the possibility of armed conflict between them. That is not a goal within our immediate grasp in respect of the Soviet Union; and we shall not bring it nearer – perhaps the very reverse – by acting prematurely as though it were. We simply cannot now see when or quite how it might be attained; it may lie a very long time off, perhaps even beyond most of our lifetimes. Meanwhile, we must seek by arms control and diplomacy to reduce the nuclear armouries of deterrence, which are needlessly large, and the nuclear costs of deterrence, which are needlessly high. If in addition we wish to improve our conventional forces – that is, in the jargon, raise the nuclear threshold – then that is fine, so long as we recognise

153

that this may be expensive in money and manpower and that it still cannot make nuclear weapons unnecessary. All these things may in some degree ease and lighten our current condition. But only international justice and freedom and openness and trust, real and not just rhetorical, can radically transform it; and there, in my view, is where Christian goals must lie. I personally cannot believe or accept that the system of deterrence – security based on keeping profound adversaries apart by the fear of monstrous disaster – is how mankind must be content to live out the rest of earthly history; we must try to find a better way in safety. But to claim that we have established such a way already would be a pretence, and a very dangerous pretence.

We can all legitimately wish that the world we live in were different; we can indeed work and pray to make it different, to create in effect a new alternative. But it will not be made different easily or quickly, and least of all by imagining that simply wishing makes it so. Meanwhile, we have for today to face the choices set us by the world as it is, the world where weapons technology and European geography and the Soviet system are what they are. In that world we of the West have to choose between having nuclear weapons and not having them, between nuclear deterrence and nuclear renunciation, asking ourselves which of them is more likely to serve peace and freedom and justice, the goals which all Christians share. It is not an easy decision, and I am deeply wary of sweeping certainties loftily dismissive of contrary views. But we do have as individuals to decide where we stand on the ethical issue. For my own part, I recognise the sincerity and commitment of those who view renunciation as an unconditional moral imperative, but for the reasons I have tried to explain I believe them to be mistaken. That is why I have been ready, and would be ready again, to work for peace through deterrence.